THE RIGHT WAY TO WRITE A CHRISTIAN BOOK

PROFESSIONALLY WRITE YOUR CHRISTIAN BOOK IN 35 DAYS OR LESS

REMNANT WRITERS™ PROFESSIONAL WRITING COURSE

TIFFANY KAMENI

THE RIGHT WAY TO WRITE A CHRISTIAN BOOK

Professionally Write Your Christian Book in 35 Days or Less!

©Tiffany Buckner-Kameni

All rights reserved. No part of this publication may be reproduced, distributed, or transmitted in any form or by any means, including photocopying, recording, or other electronic or mechanical methods, without the prior written permission of the publisher, except in the case of brief quotations embodied in critical reviews and certain other noncommercial uses permitted by copyright law. For permission requests, write to the publisher, addressed "Attention: Tiffany Kameni," at the email address below.

Anointed Fire
Email: info@anointedfire.com
www.anointedfire.com

ISBN-10: 0989756076

ISBN-13: 978-0-9897560-7-5

REMNANT WRITERS
PROFESSIONAL WRITING COURSE

The Five Week Plan

Believe it or not, the five week plan is for beginners. After you have started writing consistently for a while, you will learn how to write books in four weeks, three weeks, two weeks or maybe one week. I know one week seems far-fetched, but I can write a forty to sixty page book (in Word document 8x11 format) in seven days. How so? It's simple mathematics: If I want to write a sixty page document in seven days, I have to commit to writing around nine pages a day for six days, and on the seventh day, I would write six pages. This means I would have to be fully committed to writing and completing the book; no excuses allowed. For me, I found that I could easily do this in the late night hours, because the husband is sleeping and I'm not receiving anymore business or personal calls during that time.

Let's get one thing straight: the book will not write itself. This is not some magic book that teaches you how to say a special prayer to make a book suddenly appear. This guide is to teach you what to do and what not to do when writing a book. Additionally, this guide will teach you how to write a book in as little as five weeks. Ultimately, the completion of your book is going to depend on you. Completing your book will require dedication and determination. If you give up easily and start procrastinating, you won't finish the course or the book. This course is designed for diligence; that's the only way it works.

I would like you to set a goal of writing a forty to one hundred page book in five weeks. Please review the chart below.

Dedication

I dedicate this book to the many of you out there who are working diligently for the LORD. I applaud you for obeying GOD, and I celebrate you for wanting to write the book HE gave you the right way.

Preface

I wrote *The Right Way to Write a Christian Book* because there is a need for this information. After having read, edited and published so many Christian books, I couldn't bear standing by for another second. I'd seen my fair share of poorly written books; books written by good people who simply didn't know how to write a book. I searched the Internet for books to help these writers, but what I found was there were many books geared at helping writers in general, but there weren't many geared at helping Christian writers. General writing information isn't thorough enough for the Christian author; therefore, I decided to take action.

GOD laid it on my heart to start a company called Remnant Writers, where I'd teach Christian authors how to write best-seller material. My first class had a total of ten students in it, and I was excited knowing that ten authors would publish their books the right way. I continued the course, took the information I taught and decided to publish it for the public to access. After all, many can't afford to take the Remnant Writer's course, so I wanted to make it available to the public at an affordable rate.

The purpose of this writing course is to teach authors the proper way of writing a Christian book. In this course, I highlight the most common author errors that I have found in more than eighty percent of the books I've edited or published.

Introduction to the Professional Writing Course

The Remnant Writer's Professional Writing Course is an information-packed program that teaches first-time Christian authors the dos and don'ts of writing a book. In this program, you will learn how to write a book in as little as five weeks!

Here's the issue. Most first-time authors make a laundry list of mistakes because they do not know what it is to write a book just yet. After all, we all come into new roles with perceptions of what is expected of us to fill those roles. Because of these perceptions, we often fall prey to our own misunderstandings, and our books pay the ultimate price. You don't have to be in that percentage of self-published bloopers. Instead, in this course, you will learn to write books like a professional, and you will learn how to do so in as little as five weeks! Please be advised that it is imperative that you have your mind made up to follow the instructions. Some people come into the program dealing with the strongholds of procrastination, and they allow these strongholds to cause them to procrastinate mid-program. You have to be absolutely determined to follow this program through and through; otherwise, even though the program could work for you, it will not work since you refuse to work for yourself. This is a hands-on program full of priceless nuggets that you will use over the course of your writing career.

Also be advised that as a Christian author, it is wise for you to pray over yourself and your book. Many Christian authors go under attack from the enemy when they start to write the books GOD has graced them to write. These attacks can be prevented by:

- **Prayer.**
- **Speaking over yourself and your**

book.
- **Not blowing the trumpet and telling everyone that you are writing a book.**

Table of Contents

Dedication..III
Preface..V
Introduction to the Professional Writing Course...........VII
    The Five Week Plan..13
    The Accountability Partner.......................................21
    The Layout...25
    Until You Do Write By Me..37
    More Don'ts To Do By..43
    Excuse Calendar..73
    Tools You'll Need...77
    Starting Your Book...79
    Interviews and Surveys..93
    Common First-Time Author Errors..........................109
    Overcoming Writer's Block......................................125
    Finding the Right Words..143
    Writing Strategies 151
    Obstacles and Errors...159
    Book Professionalism..167
    Locating Your Target Audience................................181
    How to Make Money Selling Your Books................185
    Where to Make Money Selling Your Books............195
    Publishing Options...199
    Editing Your Book..203
    Reading Along or Reading Alone............................215
    Thickening Up Your Book..221
    Right Font, Wrong Attitude......................................227
    10 More No-Nos Worth Mentioning.........................233
    Professional Photography & Its Counterparts........243
    Warning About "New" Opportunities on the Block..255
    Tips For Writing a Great Fictional Book..................271
    Your Self-Published Problem 281
    Faking a Climax..303
    Helpful Links..315
    Excerpt from The Golden Book of Selling and
    Marketing Books..317

The Five Week Plan

Page Count	Weeks	Pages Per Week
40	5	8
50	5	10
60	5	12
70	5	14
80	5	16
90	5	18
100	5	20

As you can see from the chart, writing a book in five weeks is doable. You just have to commit to writing a certain amount of pages per day. Let's say you wanted to write five days out of the week. The chart below will show you how many pages you need to write each day.

Page Count	Weeks	Pages Per Day
40	5	2 pages/ day for 3 days 1 page a day for 2 days
50	5	2 pages/ day for 5 days
60	5	3 pages/ day for

The Five Week Plan

		four days
70	5	3 pages/ day for 4 days & 2 pages on final day
80	5	4 pages/ day for 4 days
90	5	4 pages/ day for 4 days & 2 pages on final day
100	5	4 pages/ day for 5 days

Of course, if you write more than five days out of the week, you can cut down on the amount of pages you are required to write per day. If you are a person who loves to write and can easily push out five pages a day, I say go for the one hundred page book. That way, once the book is formatted, you'll be looking at a book of around 150-200 pages, depending on the size of the book. If you are a person who hates to write, and writing is a struggle for you, I say go for the forty page book initially.

Also, be aware that you don't have to follow the per page numbers as listed in the chart. You can break it down however you like to. For example, if you can knock ten pages out in a day, do so. If you wanted a one hundred page book in five weeks, you could easily write five pages a day for four days out of the week instead of the four pages a day for five days as mentioned in the chart. If you wanted to write more, you could write ten pages a day for two days out of the week. Again, it all depends on you as a writer. What is too much for you? For some people, one page a day is a struggle; whereas, for others, ten pages a day is a breeze. It all depends on the following:

- Your knowledge on the subject you are writing about
- Your passion for the subject you are writing about
- Your passion for writing
- Your determination to finish the book

The Five Week Plan

I strongly advise against procrastinating and letting your pages add up; otherwise, you will become overwhelmed and abandon the program. A lot of people let their pages add up because they don't feel like writing a particular day, their favorite shows came on, or they were feeling discouraged. What ends up happening is day four comes around, for example, and they were supposed to have written two pages a day for five days. They have only written two pages total for the week. This means they have to write a total of eight pages to complete before the closing of the week; that's four pages per day. If getting two pages a day out of them was a struggle, getting four pages out of them will be a war. It always looks like a breeze until you wake up that morning with other things on your mind.

Remember, it takes 17-21 days to establish a habit. Right now, you have a habit of not writing, but you are trying to establish a habit of writing. If you follow this program through and through, you should have a habit by the time you are finished, and your second book will be a breeze. Don't give up, don't quit and don't make excuses. Just write!

The Accountability Partner

While taking this course, it would be best if you had an accountability partner, or several accountability partners. The reason for this is that most first-time authors battle procrastination and are trying to push past the strongholds that have kept them from writing for years. When left up to their own devices, they'll treat this program the way most people (including myself) treat a diet; they'll start off good and end up back where they started.

Even better is if your accountability partner helped you to pay for this program and they are taking it as well. That's because most people do not respect what they did not pay for. Having two or more soon-to-be authors engaging one another and holding one another accountable helps to increase the chance that the author won't give up mid-program.

How can an accountability partner help you? It's simple: They can help you by pushing, encouraging and penalizing you for your actions or lack thereof.

The Push: Most of us need a push. Your accountability partner can push you by checking in on your progress and cheering you along the way.

The Encouragement: Encouragement is just an emotional push. Sometimes, we simply need loving reminders of who we are and who we serve.

Penalty: Honestly, this is my favorite because I can be pretty stubborn. A push may work for one person, encouragement may work for another, but for me, I often need penalties to put a little fire underneath my wings. Penalties can include: Five dollars paid to your favorite charity for every day you didn't write, or bothersome chores added to your daily roster. Always make sure that any penalty you give yourself is not one that you want. Even though charities are great, most people want to give only a select amount of money to a charity; therefore, giving more than they intended may become bothersome to them. That's why it's a great way to train the mind. You are helping someone else, and at the same time, you are proactively making an effort to write and complete your book. When you do this consistently, you will find that your mind will slowly change, and after a while, you will write without having to be threatened with self-imposed penalties.

The Layout

There are many things that first-time authors often neglect to do because they are first-time authors. When you know better, you'll do better; we all know this. But there are authors who purposely avoid going through the necessary steps because they are either eager to publish their books, or they don't want to do the work involved. I found this especially true with Christian authors; nevertheless, as you mature as an author and get a few books under your belt, you will find that laying out your book properly is a saver of time and money, and it'll save you from the frustration of having a book with no layout.

First off, you need to create an outline for your book. Ordinarily, you will need the following, so go ahead and create pages for them:

The Layout

- **Title Page**- The title page is just a page where you will list your book's title, subtitle and your name as the author.

- **Copyright Page**- The copyright page is the page where you will list your book's copyright, year the book was copy-written and your book's disclaimer. The book's copyright page also contains the ISBN number, edition number of the book and publisher's information.

- **Dedication**- A dedication page is simply a page where you list who you are dedicating the book to. For example, spouses often list their spouse's names, parents often list their children, and of course, many people list the LORD.

- **Acknowledgment**- An acknowledgment page is simply a page where the author acknowledges the people who have helped him or her with the writing,

The Layout

production or marketing of the book. It is a "thank you" note to everyone involved.

- **Table of Content**- The table of content is a guide to finding each chapter. It lists the chapter name and the page number the chapter starts on.

- **Foreword**- A foreword is a message written by someone else other than the author. It usually shows a relationship between the author and the person writing the foreword. The foreword is basically the writer's way of vouching for the author and the author's book. Forewords are often written by other authors, and authors often seek out best-sellers or well-known figures to do their forewords.

- **Preface**- A preface is written in the author's own words, firsthand. It is the author detailing the reason they wrote the book, what inspired them to write or any events that led up to the conception of the book.

- **Introduction**- An introduction is a summary of what's covered in the book. It's like window shopping: the reader gets a chance to get a little bit of an understanding in relation to what the book is about, the characters involved and the tone of the book.

You do not have to absolutely have all of these pages. As a matter of fact, every page is optional except for the title page and the table of content.

Go ahead and create a table of content, listing at least ten chapters to be written on. I'll explain why a little bit into the book. Also list the table of content in your planner, and be

The Layout

sure to list any quotes or scriptures you'd like to feature on the top of each page. After you've done that, list at least three to five topics to be discussed in that particular chapter. Here's an example:

Table of Content

What is Depression

- Webster's dictionary definition of depression as well as the Bible's definition

- My battle with depression and what the doctor told me

- The root causes of depression

- Facts and statistics about depression and their after-effects

The Devil Behind Depression

- The spirits associated with depression

- The strongholds of depression and their

aim

- Man's version of what depression is versus the scriptural meaning

Signs of Depression

- List symptoms of depression
- List behaviors associated with depression
- Share my story about how I first came to recognize I was in this stronghold
- Interview five to ten people who were either clinically diagnosed with depression or basically realized they were depressed. List how they overcame

Overcoming Depression

- The first steps to healing: recognition, acknowledgment and confrontation
- Scriptures readers should memorize

and quote for deliverance

- What is to be expected during the fight and dealing with backsliding
- Taming the mind to tap into the joy of the LORD

As you can see from the table of content, the author pretty much laid out the groundwork for their book. All they have to do from here is follow through. This makes writing the book so much easier than trying to wing it page-to-page.

Drafting Your Book

Next, you need to write your first draft. Now, understand that a first draft doesn't mean that you jot down notes and list important pointers to add to the final copy. Your book's draft is actually your book in progress. It is in its infancy stage, and you are having to dress it up and then clean it up before you send it out.

With the first draft, you just write the book: that's it. Be careful that you are not throwing something together with no outline or formatting; otherwise, you'll end up having to go back and clean the book up. Believe it or not, cleaning up a book can take as much, if not more, time than writing a book. View the wrong and right way examples below:

Wrong way:

As a Christian, you should own land for many reasons.

-Because the earth is the LORD'S and the fullness thereof. (List scripture later)

-Scripture about HE will give us houses that we didn't build....

-Earthly authority over the land gives you spiritual authority.

-"A good *man* leaveth an inheritance to his children's children: and the wealth of the sinner *is* laid up for the just" (Proverbs 13:22).

The Layout

As you can see, the author writing the book the wrong way has his/her work cut out for him/her. They have to actually go back and write the book, and this process can be tedious, excruciating and time-consuming when you've written over one hundred pages. Let's review the right way.

Right Way:

As Christians, we should own land for many reasons, and they include:

- Because the earth is the LORD'S and the fullness thereof. (*See Psalms 24:1*)

- Because it is our inheritance! *"And I have given you a land for which ye did not labour, and cities which ye built not, and ye dwell in them; of the vineyards and oliveyards which ye planted not do ye eat" (Joshua 24:13).*

- Earthly authority over the land gives you spiritual authority over the land.

The Layout

- *"A good man leaveth an inheritance to his children's children: and the wealth of the sinner is laid up for the just"* (Proverbs 13:22).

In the wrong way example, the author made several mistakes.

1. The author did tell the reader that he or she was about to list the reasons to own land.

2. The author used dashes instead of bullet points. Dashes work mid-sentence or behind a title, but dashes are not to start off a pointer. Instead, to list points, you should always use bullet points or numbers. You can use standard numbering or roman numerals, if you choose to use numbers.

3. The author did not list what scriptures he or she was taking notes from. Instead, the author left himself/ herself a

note to add the scriptures later. This will prove to be time-consuming, and many authors actually overlook these little notations when they publish their books, especially those who didn't hire editors. It is better to go ahead and list the scriptures, pointers and so on, instead of planning to do it later. Remember, your book is not the best place to jot down notes; you have a notepad for that.

4. If the author plans to highlight scriptures a certain way, he or she didn't do it in the initial draft. This often causes poorly written books to be published because it's not easy to go back through a book and find tedious errors. Oftentimes, authors will go back and find 98 percent of the scriptures and highlight them, but they'll miss the other two percent. If you do this from the start, however, it will not end up as a problem for you.

Edit As You Go

As you write the book, go back and reread what you have written as you go along. I recommend reading yesterday's text today and reading today's text tomorrow. That way you won't breeze through it. Remember, you are your first book's editor. Even if you aren't a great speller, or if you aren't great with punctuation, you will still be able to catch some errors when you reread your book.

Until You Do Write By Me

There are a few writing rules that journalists and authors write by. If you are a first-time author, and you've never written articles or done any type of journalism, chances are you don't know these rules. But they will help you along your writing route so you can jump over the term "rookie" writer and go straight into being a professional writer.

1. Write any numbers under ten out. For example, number one should not be written as number 1, number two should not be written as number 2, and so on.
2. Write even numbers out, even when they are over ten. For example, 60 should be written as sixty, 100 should be written as one hundred, and 1,000

should be written as one thousand. Uneven numbers over ten should be written in numeral format, however.

3. Never start off a sentence with a numeral. Instead, the number should be written out.
   Wrong Way: "12 years ago, Billy married Barbara."
   Right Way: "Twelve years ago, Billy married Barbara."
4. When writing two numerals side-by-side, always list one number and spell the other one out. Example: "Five 3-year-old children were at Meghan's party."
5. When using ordinal numbers such as first and second, spell the words out; do not list them as 1st and 2nd.
6. When writing percentiles, always list the words and not the symbols. For example, you should not write 15%; instead, you should write 15 percent.

7. Never use two negative statements to make a positive statement. For example: "Jerry was not unfair to her." The correct way to write this is: "Jerry was fair to her."

8. Take it easy on the exclamation points. This is especially important for Christian writers, since some writers tend to get emotional while writing. You should use exclamation points sparingly. Try to only use one exclamation point every three pages if you must have them. Don't list several to express how powerful the message is to you; let your readers be the judge. Wrong way: "Elizabeth was furious!!!!!!" Right way: "Elizabeth was furious." Wrong way: "Our GOD is an awesome GOD!!!!!!!" Right way: "Our GOD is an awesome GOD!" Remember this: People don't often get "happy" reading books, and they do NOT hear

you when you write.

9. Use your active voice, not your passive voice. Every sentence has a subject, and the subject should be the one in action. Wrong way: "Melvin was cared for by Joanne." Right way: "Joanne cared for Melvin." Writing should read as if you are giving a police report, not riding along in a vehicle with your reader.

10. Spell it out. Remember "etc." stands for et cetera, and it means the following:
- "and so on"
- "and so forth"
- "and other things"

You should never use etc. in a book; instead, spell it out. Wrong way: "Joyce burned the coffee, the food, John's shirt, etc." Right way: "Joyce burned the coffee, the food and John's shirt, amongst other things.

11. Don't over-punctuate a sentence. I see this done in many Christian books, and it is wrong, wrong, wrong! Sentences that require excessive punctuation should be broken up into more than one sentence. Wrong way: "Janet told her mom, her aunt and her co-workers that she would no longer work the morning shift, but she forgot to tell her husband, so he was pretty upset with her; therefore, he didn't speak to her at breakfast, lunch and dinner." That's a lengthy sentence, and it may be confusing to the reader. Right way: "Janet told her mom, aunt and co-workers that she would no longer work the morning shift, but she forgot to tell her husband. Because of this, her husband did not speak to her at breakfast, lunch and dinner."

More Don'ts To Do By

There are a few things that if left unsaid will become a snare for a few authors. Of course, many of the tips listed are common knowledge; but then again, everyone is not common.

There are a few things you should NOT do when writing a book, and I'll list a few of them so you won't end up stumbling over them.

1. Do not write your book manually (pen and paper). I have come across quite a few authors who have done this, and their first question to me (as a publisher) is if we can put their handwritten document in book format. Of course, I had to inform them that they would have to take their three hundred page written

documents and actually type them out or end up paying someone to do so. I have yet to find one author who has been happy upon hearing this. All the same, I have yet to find one author who has actually followed through with publishing their books after they heard what people charge to transcribe their documents from written to print.

2. Do not save your books on a public access computer. If you don't have access to your own personal computer, it is better to save your document to a USB drive when using a public access computer (i.e. library, college or internet cafe). Someone may take what you have written so far and turn it in as their term paper.

3. Don't use slashes (/) to substitute as words unless it is absolutely necessary. You can use slashes when you are

writing "him/her", but it is better to write it out as "him or her" or "him and her". The only time you should use slashes is when your sentence has the word "and" or the word "or" used multiple times. You should also use a slash when you are giving the option of and/or.

Wrong Way: "You should consider going to dancing school with your kids. They have a section for boys/girls."

Right Way: "You should consider going to dancing school with your kids. They have a section for both boys and girls."

Wrong Way: "Sarah didn't know who had taken her food from the refrigerator.

4. Write the book. Don't jot down notes and call it a book. I have met countless authors who have told me that they have books they have written, but there is one problem: they don't actually have "books" per se, they have pages of

notes they have jotted down. They intend to transform these notes into books, but it hasn't happened yet. The reason people procrastinate on changing the notes into an actual book is because it takes too much time! The time spent jotting down notes could have been the time spent actually elaborating on those notes. It's great to take notes; don't mistake what I'm saying. The issue is when you don't write the book; instead, you take notes and plan to write the book. What comes forward is documents upon documents of text that end up serving as a discouragement to the author because of the document size. If you have thirty pages of notes, you're likely not going to write the book because it's all too overwhelming. Jot down notes when you don't have time to write, but

whenever you get a free moment, go and elaborate on the notes you have jotted down while they are still fresh.
5. Don't just save one copy; save multiple copies of your book file on several USB drives and/or computers. The worst thing for any author to experience is to lose their USB drives and have no access to the books they have written. There are actually authors who have written multiple books and saved them to their USB, only to lose them. Of course, this is overwhelming for any author; therefore, be sure to have at least two copies on hand.
6. If you are writing a fiction book or novel, don't tell people about your characters and what you will have them to do. People need to feel as if the characters are real, and they need to be surprised at the actions of the characters.

More Don'ts to Do By

Knowing that this is something you are conjuring up takes the realness out of it and actually may cost you some readers. Keep quiet and write the book.

7. When giving a testimony, don't use the actual names of the people involved. If you do, you are likely to be sued for defamation of character, should your book become a best-seller. Even if you are writing positive stories about the people you know, be sure to ask their permission and have them sign a disclaimer giving you permission to use their names. Remember, you can always use a fictitious name; it is not mandatory that you use actual names.

8. Don't jump from book to book. Finish what you are writing first. If you are like me, you may have several books you are working at any given time. GOD may give you an idea for one book, and

just as you are writing that book, HE gives you another one to write. In that case, you should open up a new document and write down whatever HE has given you; nevertheless, once the notes have dried up, go back to the book you are writing until the LORD gives you more for the second book. Now, there are some times when the LORD may have you stop midway through a book to complete another book, and this is okay. Always obey what the LORD tells you to do, but don't obey your flesh. There will be times when you may prefer to write in another book rather than completing the one you have been writing in. Oftentimes, this is because the book you are writing in is starting to pull on you, require that you research more, and it's making you tap in to a time that you don't want to tap into. This actually means you have gotten into the heart of the book; it's not a time to give up and start another book. Again, obey what GOD tells you to do, but do NOT give in to your flesh.

9. Do not compromise your book for any reason. As a Christian author, you will often find yourself feeling convicted about writing certain things in your book. That's because the enemy doesn't want to be exposed; therefore, he will accuse you and attempt to convict you into submission. Don't give in to this; instead, let it push you to go more in depth with what you are writing.

10. Being disrespectful and condemning does not make for a good read. Do not spend your time chastising a certain group of people; otherwise, you may come off as self-righteous and judgmental. It goes without saying that

when you tell the truth, there will be people who feel judged and there is nothing you can do about this. Nevertheless, there are many authors who cross the line between telling the truth and being offensive. For example, review the two sentences below.

Wrong Way: "A woman who engages in fornication is a whore; that's biblical. There are so many women who will lay down for just about anyone, and then they wonder why they have a bunch of illegitimate children with no father. Then they have the nerve to get upset with the dad of the child because he doesn't want to pay child support. What do you expect? You gave him free sex!"

Right Way: "The bible defines a whoremonger (whore) as a woman who sleeps with more than one man; nevertheless, society has redefined the term "whore" to mean a woman who sleeps with more than five men in a year's time. In this day and age, there are so many women who don't know their worth; therefore, they submit their bodies to men who have no intentions of being their husbands. As a result, children are born to one-parent households where the dad is absent, and this can be hurtful to any child. The mother of these children, having seen the hurt and disappointment on their children's faces, is often upset with the father of these children because they are not there to help rear them. In doing so, the mother diminishes her responsibility in the act that left her children fatherless. She is also upset that the father does not want to pay child support, and this anger is justifiable; nevertheless, both parties have shared responsibility in their children's misery."

As you can see, the Right Way is less offensive and speaks of the problem. Because it's not degrading or profane in its tone, it may actually help both men and women; whereas the Wrong Way gives off a self-righteous tone. Instead of helping women to discover their value, it comes off as a group of self-righteous women standing in a hurdle judging anyone who is not like them.

11. Do not keep sentences, paragraphs and pages that don't read well. As an author, you will have those times when you reread a paragraph or a page, and it'll just sound awful to you. But the problem arises that you don't want to get rid of the text; after all, you have written hours and hours of text, and you don't want to delete it. You will read this

pointer over and over again in this book: delete it! The worst thing you can do to a good book is to leave it littered with bad paragraphs.

12. Pay attention to whom you focus on as you are writing. Don't focus the message as if you are writing to the wrong-doers; otherwise, your message will be full of condemnation and negativity. Instead, focus on those who want to be helped; after all, they are the ones who will likely buy your book. People who don't want help won't seek it. If you are writing a book to help men become better fathers, it would be wise to focus on the men who want to be better fathers. It is unwise to focus your entire book on deadbeat dads because the message is one of negativity. It's okay to point out the toll that an absent father has on his children; howbeit, it is

better to focus on the positive effects a present father has. This encourages men to want to be present in their children's lives, whereas the condemning book reads like a nagging woman on a rainy day.

13. Don't try to convince others of your Christianity. Oftentimes, authors go on and on about what they do for the LORD; how they love the LORD and what HE has done for them, but they leave the readers out. So, the readers end up reading a book where the main subject is the author and the author's relationship with the LORD. If it's not a biography about yourself that you have written, your readers aren't going to want to hear you go on and on about your relationship with the LORD, how you overcame your "haters" and what GOD has promised you.

More Don'ts to Do By

14. Don't use run-on sentences. Knowing when to end a sentence is very important. A run-on sentence is a sentence that consists of two independent clauses. Instead of the writer dividing the clauses, they attempt to join them in one sentence, and this is error. An example of a run-on sentence is: "Joel ran for mayor he lost the race." The correct way to write this sentence is: "Joel ran for mayor and lost the race." Or you can write it as: "Joe ran for mayor. He lost the race." Sentences that can stand by themselves should stand by themselves or be conjoined by commas, apostrophes and conjunctive words such as and, but or however. Another bad example is: "Maria wants to learn to speak French Jason wants to learn Spanish." As you can see, the above sentence should be divided

because it doesn't make sense the way it is. Better example: "Maria wants to learn to speak French, but Jason wants to learn Spanish." Both clauses were joined by the word "but". It could also be written as: "Maria wants to learn to speak French, however, Jason wants to learn Spanish." The sentence could also be divided up into two sentences: "Maria wants to learn to speak French. Jason wants to learn Spanish."

15. Avoid writing sentence fragments. A sentence fragment is basically an incomplete sentence. A sentence must have a subject, a verb and a complete idea. An example of a sentence fragment is: "The mountain lion chewed." What did the mountain lion chew? Another example is: "Tammy told me." What did Tammy tell you? Oftentimes, authors incorporate

fragments after the completion of a sentence because they are attempting to write the same way they speak. For example, someone may verbally say, "Gregory was being inconsiderate of Melissa's condition. He asked for it." What did Gregory ask for? What is "it"? Sentences are statements that should include a subject, verb and complete idea. Remember, you should never write the same way you speak.

16. Writing a book is not the same as updating your Facebook status. Don't try to stir everyone up with a message; instead, write as GOD leads you to write. Don't intentionally try to make people emotional. Let the Word of the LORD touch their hearts.

17. When writing a prophetic message, always make sure not to include yourself. Oftentimes, Christian writers

put too much of themselves into the prophecy. Example: "I hear the LORD saying...." or "The LORD told me to tell you...." Prophecy is prophecy and only the message should be conveyed. You do not have to let the readers know that you are a Prophet, or you have the gift of prophecy; instead, just convey the message. A good way to convey the message should read:

Prophecy: (Dated: 10/18/2013)
Message from the LORD: ....

As you write, you can stop and add prophecies as GOD gives them to you, but remove yourself from the prophecies. All too often, authors try to incorporate themselves, and this tone may not be received well by readers. They know that you are writing the book; therefore, GOD is obviously speaking to and through you. They can draw a conclusion from there.

18. Never use statements like:

"Trust me."

"You don't know me."

"They didn't know me."

"If you knew me."

"One thing about me..."

People who like to read aren't interested in all of the references to "me" that people throw in their books, unless the book is a biography. When someone opens a biography, they are intentionally trying to read about you. When they open a self-help book, they are intentionally trying to find help, not you. It is a great thing to add testimonies in your self-help books. In these cases, you aren't adding "you" to the message; instead, "you" have become a part of the message. Don't keep redirecting the readers' eyes from the message to yourself and then back to the message. Think of it this way: If you went to a friend's house crying about a situation you were in; would you like it if she took you to the mirror to show you how beautiful you are, but she ends up being distracted by her own reflection? That's what it's like to read a self-help book where the author doesn't help out much, but keeps pointing their words at themselves.

19. Don't be insistent on taking credit for what you have said. Your readers know that it comes from you; after all, you are the author of the book. Example: "The greatest weapon a man has against himself is himself. Now, that is a statement I came up with a few years back." This is tacky and let's the reader know that you are insistent on pointing

the spotlight at yourself, even in your own book.

20. Make your point, but don't stay there! Make your point and move on to the next point; don't keep circling around what you've already said. Some authors have absolutely nothing to say, so they keep saying the same thing over and over again in different words. An example is: "As a woman, you should never go walking when it's dark outside. There are many predators who like the cover of darkness, and they love to find a single woman walking by herself. Walking at nighttime opens exposes you as a woman. It is not a good idea to walk at night when you are a woman because it's dangerous. There are many people who like to prey on the vulnerable. Because you are a woman, you are on a predator's wish list." As

you can see, the author keeps circling around the same message. This is a no-no when writing; nevertheless, this is **very** common with Christian writers.

21. Don't write a question and then answer it. Example: "Can someone tell me why politics are so hard to understand? I can! It's because politicians are hard to understand." The better way to write this is: "I can tell you why politics are so hard to understand. It is because politicians are hard to understand." All the same, don't ask readers to raise their hands to answer a question you have asked. I have seen this in books, and it is tacky. Example: "Do you know the distance between Russia and China? Can anyone answer that question? What? You mean to tell me no one can answer it? Okay, well, I guess I have to answer it. The distance

between Russia and China is over thirty-six hundred miles!" Your readers cannot participate in this; therefore, you should never invite them to answer a question that they have no way of responding to. It is also tacky for you to turn around and answer your own question.

22. Don't answer a question that hasn't been asked. Example: "Yes, my dog had fleas, and I had to have him treated." What is the purpose of starting the sentence with "yes"? Another tacky example is: "I'm sure you want to know why you are in pain, so I will answer you." The readers didn't ask that question, so why are you answering them? At the same time, most readers don't appreciate the use of the word "you" in relation to things negative. The correct way is to say, for example: "Many people are in pain because......"

More Don'ts to Do By

23. Don't ask the readers to engage in any acts or shout out any words. This is common with Pastors and leaders, but it should **not** be done. Example: "Somebody shout hallelujah, and give JESUS a crazy praise!" What happens when the reader doesn't do it, or if they don't feel like it? Will the earth open up and swallow them? When someone requests an act; especially in a Christian book, many readers end up feeling condemned, or they do things that they don't want to do because they don't want to be in disobedience. Remember, they may be at work, hiding in their cubicles and attempting to quietly read your book. They aren't going to shout nor will they appreciate your attempt to rouse them. Another example: "Can I get an amen?"

24. Don't tell the readers what you are about

to do behind a comment. Just write and teach them. Example: "I just preached myself into a corner. I'm about to go and get some water behind that one! I had to run around my room after that!"

25. Don't tell your readers what you have done behind a comment. Don't tell your readers what you are physically doing....period! Example: "That word was so good that I almost fell out of my chair!" Another example: "I'm back. I had to stop and praise the LORD for a minute. I felt that one in my bones!" Readers don't need to know that you took a break. It's tacky! Just write the message that you are teaching.

26. Don't tell readers how you feel. It's tacky! Example: "I can feel the glory of GOD as I type this message! Whew!" Why do they need to know that you felt the glory of GOD? Will it add substance

to your book? When telling readers how you feel, you distract the readers from the message and bring their mental focus on you and what you are doing at the moment. They end up imagining you dancing around your computer and shouting. For them, this serves as a poorly inserted commercial break, and they have to wait to get back to the regularly scheduled reading.

27. Don't write as if you are answering the LORD. It's tacky! Example: "I can feel GOD as I type this message! Oh, glory! Yes, LORD; I hear you! Yes, LORD! Okay, so this is what HE is saying..." GOD can hear your voice, so why write what you want to say? Writers who do this are attempting to prove themselves to the readers; instead, they come off as phony, arrogant and attention-starved.

28. Never write vague comments or refer to

previous text, chapters or paragraphs vaguely. Don't make your readers have to review previous paragraphs trying to figure out what you are talking about. It's tacky! Example: "Okay, so back to what we were talking about earlier. It's as if Margaret knew Steve would find her journal, so she made the right decision to hide it. What Steve read angered him, but he had no right to be upset. After all, Margaret hadn't done anything wrong." What's going on here? The reader may find themselves lost. To catch up, they have to go back and reread previous paragraphs, or in some cases, previous chapters. This is tacky! You have to remind the readers of the entire story. You don't have to tell the story again, but you have to remind them of the important points. Example: "Do you understand how watching too much television is not good for the Christian? This goes with the point I made earlier. Watching too much television is distracting and can become a Christian's only source for information." What just happened here? I need to know the point the author made earlier; therefore, I may have to go back and research it just to catch up.

29. Remember not to convey this message: I'm saved, but you need help. Readers hate books where the writer writes as if they have figured it out and are saved, but the reader needs direction. All too often, authors involve themselves in the good, all the while condemning the readers unintentionally. Example: "I love GOD and HE hears me. HE loves me too and we have a great relationship. How can you not love HIM? HE'S been too good to me for me not to praise HIM!

You can continue serving yourself, those false gods and your money, but as for me and my house, we will serve the LORD!" Can you see how such text could be a turn off to the reader? It's like you invited them to a parade of "me", but they were arrested for not being you.

30. Don't pretend to be perfect. Believe it or not, your readers know better. Take ownership of your wrongs before showing someone else their shortcomings. Again, remember to avoid self-righteous tones. Readers love to know that whatever they are struggling with, you have struggled with, or at least you know someone who struggled and overcame that same yoke. Never present yourself as spotless, or you make the reader feel tainted and beneath you, and they often

More Don'ts to Do By

lash out in response.

Excuse Calendar

What is an excuse calendar? The excuse calendar was developed to help writers to see their strongholds or the overcoming of their strongholds in plain sight. What you do with the excuse calendar is document every day that you did not write and list your excuse on the calendar. The next day, you should double up on your work, and if another excuse rises up, record it. Pay attention to your habits. They will often tell you if you are dealing with a stronghold, whereas you can't seem to push past your feelings to write your book.

Also, use the assignment book to write notes to yourself, motivating yourself and listing the reasons you don't feel like writing some days. What you are doing is addressing yourself and your mindset. You are challenging yourself to write and not giving in to the excuses that once held you prisoner.

For every excuse you publish on your calendar, be sure to write yourself a note detailing what you could have done and what you will do the next time the issue arises. I know this advice is unconventional, but you are a peculiar being; you can't push past mentalities with practical advice. Finally, be sure to penalize yourself. This makes the problem real to you, and helps you to drown out of the noise of your flesh.

Also, please note that there are tons of excuses that writers use. Anyone can just pick an excuse and stop writing, but oftentimes less than fifty percent of would-be authors push past themselves to go ahead and write the books GOD has given them to write. The ones who do not push past themselves often find some of the most creative and elaborate excuses to justify going back under their strongholds. The most common justification is: "It's probably not my season to write." Now, this is after people have said that GOD has been strongly dealing with them about writing whatever book HE has given them to write.

Another thing that often happens with Christian writers is they go under attack when they decide to go ahead and obey GOD. Understand that this is to be expected. The enemy will not just sit back and watch you launch an attack against his kingdom. He will put up some resistance. After all, a book given to you by GOD can possibly help millions of souls to get set free. While under attack, more than fifty percent of writers retreat, planning to write on sunnier days. That's why I advise would-be authors to pray over themselves, their writings and their plans. At the same time, if you find yourself coming under attack, don't let it cause you to run away. Make the devil run away. *"Submit yourselves therefore to God. Resist the devil, and he will flee from you" (James 4:7).* Know this: Sometimes what we think are attacks aren't always attacks; sometimes, it's the fire of GOD that refines us so that GOD can pull out of us what HE has put in us.

Utilize the excuse calendar to help you to get past those excuses so you can be a part of the little over forty percent who actually overcome their flesh to write some pretty powerful books. And don't for one day make an excuse as to why you didn't publish an excuse on the excuse calendar!

For the days that you do write, simply use the calendar to note how many pages you wrote that day.

Tools You'll Need

To start the Professional Writing Course, you will need the following tools:

- **Computer (Obviously)**
- **An Internet Connection-** You will need to connect to the Internet to perform certain actions.
- **Microsoft Word or Open Office-** (Any writing program where you can save the document in .doc format).
- **Notebook-** You will need a notebook to jot down notes.
- **Pen or Pencil-** Since you'll be using a notebook, you obviously need a pen or pencil to write in the notebook with.
- **The Right Way to Write a Christian Book II-** You will be using the calendar to document your accomplishments and

excuses. You will also use the journal to jot down notes and encourage yourself.

Other tools that would be great to have, but are not mandatory, include:

- **Digital Voice Recorder-** This is a great tool to have to record notes on the go.
- **Printer-** A printer is good to have to help edit your book. You'll find out how as you read more into the book.

Starting Your Book

Every author has his or her own unique way of starting a book. You will find that some authors like to conduct hours and hours of research before writing a book: some prefer to create an outline, while others prefer to just write. Below are a few tips to help you start your book.

Table of Contents

In literature class, the teacher used to give us a subject to write about. I found that this made writing easier for me than being told to just write.

Initially, when I started writing books, I would just write. This was both time-consuming and challenging, because I had to think about what the next chapter would be once I'd finish the previous chapter. Then this GOD-given idea came in from Heaven: Why not create the Table of Contents first and then go from there? It worked for me, and it works for the majority of the people that I have suggested it to. I'm sure that you know what your book is about. Let's say your book is about human trafficking in America. The goal of your book is to expose human trafficking, educate readers about human trafficking, and try to put an end to it. A great Table of Content would be:

- What is Human Trafficking?
- Human Trafficking Statistics
- Human Trafficking in America
- Interviews With Trafficking Victims
- Exposing the Faces of Human Traffickers
- Putting a Stop To Human Trafficking

The Table of Contents above gives me an outline to work with. Now I know what I need to research and write about. This makes it easier for me to just go chapter-to-chapter until I'm done. Of course, I'm not exactly stuck with the Table of Contents either. As a writer, you will often find yourself adding and deleting chapters as you go along. When I write a book, I normally create at least ten chapters to post in my Table of Contents. Normally, two of them don't make the cut, and I end up adding five to ten more as I go along. As you write, new ideas will come to you based on what you are writing. Oftentimes, you will write something in one chapter that stirs up a whole new chapter. When this happens, go ahead and populate it in your Table of Contents so you don't forget about it.

Creating an Outline

In addition to creating your Table of Contents, you need to create a basic outline for your book. This will help you remain consistent and save you money when you send your book to be edited. Be sure to decide the following, and write it down in one of your notebooks:

Pointers- Will you use bullet points, numbers or Roman numerals?

Indentation- Are you going to indent before each paragraph, and if so, how many spaces will you use before the start of each sentence?

Scriptures- How are you going to list scriptures? Will you place them in quotations, italicize them or both?

Font- What font will you use for your header text, and what font will you use for your body text? What size will be your body's text, and what size will you use for your header's text?

Bold- What objects in your text will you place a bold effect on? For example, will you bold the quotes by others, or will you bold their names only?

Interviews- How will you list interviews? Will each interview have its own page, and how will you list the dialogues? Will the names of the interviewer and interviewee be bold or underlined?

You have to have a basic outline set up; otherwise, you will forget how you are outlining your book as you go further into it. A lot of first-time authors think their editors will make these corrections, but they are wrong. A lot of first-time authors think the publisher will make these corrections, but they are wrong again. It is the author's job to write the book and set it up the way they want it to be published. It is the editor's job to edit the book, looking for and correcting errors in spelling, grammar, punctuation and sentence setup. It is the publisher's job to publish the book.

Don't Quit For Any Reason

When we hold a Remnant Writer's class, ordinarily only fifty percent of the students that come in actually write and finish their books.

The other fifty percent can't get past themselves to finish. Some people take the course believing that we will basically write the book for them. In other words, there are actually people who think we will act as ghost writers; we'll tell them what to write and how to write it. But it doesn't work that way. As an author, you have to write your own book unless you hire a ghost writer. This fact may be alarming to many readers, but that's just how authoring goes.

Then, there are those aspiring authors who think we will call them daily to check their progress. After the call, we would review their books, make suggestions and even make a few corrections for them. This is no joke; there are actually aspiring authors out there who aspire to have the "author" title without doing the work of an author. When reality sets in, and they realize they actually have to do the work, they quit. The sad part is: a few years down the road, they are still aspiring.

I write that to say this: Make sure you are serious about writing your book before you start. Understand that you won't feel like writing because you're not used to it yet; that's normal. But it takes you getting past how you feel to sit down and take the title of author by force. There will be some challenges to come your way. That's because you are a Christian author writing for the LORD. Anytime you are about to deliver a baby, you will experience labor pains. Don't think for one second that writing is a birthday party full of laughter and blissful moments. Writing makes you tap into some places you don't want to tap into. For example, you may have to recall hurt that you have endured in your life. You may have to put yourself in the shoes of someone else as you try to tell their story. You may have to endure the pain of your character as you attempt to explain to your readers what your character is experiencing and feeling. When writing a book, you will laugh and you will cry. That's when you know your book is good.

Don't give up writing that book. Make up your mind that no matter what happens, you will write and finish that book. Give yourself a date of completion and stick by it. I have to be honest with you. I don't ever recall not going under attack or not going through refining moments when I decided to write the books I have written. I went through attacks behind attacks; I was challenged on the inside to bring what was in me to the outside. I thought about giving up many times, but I couldn't do it. Many moments that we think are attacks are actually refining moments where we were tested, tried and perfected to write the books GOD has given us to write. Nevertheless, more than fifty percent of authors will let these moments define what they will and will not do, rather than letting GOD refine them.

Set Yourself a Schedule

When writing a book, you should set yourself a schedule to write every day. Writers with a schedule are more likely to complete their books than writers who do not have a schedule. All the same, printed schedules are better than memorized ones.

It is better to schedule yourself to write at least five days a week. Each day, make it a point to complete at least ten pages or one chapter in your book. When you do this, you will actually see yourself progressing towards the completion of your book. This will oftentimes serve as an encouragement to you to finish your book.

Whatever you do, do not forsake your schedule. Don't take it lightly; stick to it. You have to be a better boss of you than the boss you have at your secular job. Schedule yourself and follow through with your schedule, even when you don't want to. There will be days when you'd rather do something else. It happens to all of us. If you can't push past yourself to write on those days, you will more than likely not finish your book. If you do finish it, it may be years down the road.

Remember, you have decided that you want your book to be finished in five weeks or less. To pull off this feat, you have to write every day. I recommend writing at least ten pages a week, but if you can write more, do so. Ten pages a week for five weeks will give you fifty pages. Formatted as a 5x8, you may be looking at close to 100 pages. That's a pretty decent sized book, especially for a first-time author.

Prepare the People Around You

A change in your daily routine will often affect a change in your family's daily routine. It's hard enough for you to rearrange your schedule and your life to write a book, but it's even harder for someone on the outside to adjust to the new you. Children are especially threatened by any change they witness in their parents. Change represents the unknown, and the unknown tends to stir up fear or excitement in people. With that being said, you need to prepare your family members and friends for your new journey. Let everyone know that you will be busy every day at a certain time, and you are not to be disturbed at that time. You don't have to tell your friends or anyone outside of your home what you are doing, but you do need to make it clear to them that you will be busy. All too often people are threatened by change and will become clingy, needy or fearful when you attempt to change; especially if they have gotten used to your routine.

You will find that your children will be the most challenging when you start to write because they don't understand why you are taking time for yourself every day. Even after you have requested that your kids be quiet and mindful of what you are doing, you will probably witness them on their worst behavior whenever you sit down to write. Of course, every parent handles discipline in their own way; therefore, I can't tell you how to discipline your children. What I can say is that you need to set up rules and consequences <u>before</u> you start your writing journey. Even better than that, if you can write when the children are tucked away in bed, you may be able to flow better as a writer since you won't have the distractions.

If you are married, you should politely request that your spouse help you with the children so that you can sit down to write without distractions. Also, be sure to ask the spouse to respect your schedule. Never attempt to write with your spouse sitting next to you unless the two of you are writing together or you feel comfortable with the spouse sitting there. In many cases, the spouse may serve as a distraction and even question your choice of words. Such questioning could be discouraging to a first-time writer.

Remember to Take Breaks

When writing, there will be times when your mind will seem to shutdown, and your body will want to do something other than sitting at the computer. It's okay to take a break as long as you come back and finish your assignment for the day.

Taking breaks will often help to revitalize your mind and stir up some new ideas. Breaks don't always involve a couch, a snack and a television set; breaks can be taking fifteen minutes to an hour away from writing to research what you are writing about. It doesn't sound like a break now, but when you start to write, you will find that filling your mind with new info will often be something you welcome after you have been emptied out.

Again, it is okay to take breaks. Just make sure that you finish writing the amount of pages you scheduled yourself to write each day.

Interviews and Surveys

You will find throughout this book that I suggest to writers that they conduct interviews and surveys for various reasons. One of the reasons for this is to fluff up your book, or give it more pages. Another reason is to add depth to your book. There are many reasons you should consider conducting interviews or surveys, but ultimately, it's up to you. You need to do what is best for your book.

What's the difference between an interview and a survey? Of course, the two are not one and the same. An interview is a person-to-person meeting where one person asks the other person a list of questions. The person being questioned is the interviewee, and the person asking the questions is the interviewer. It goes without saying: most interviews conducted are published for public evaluation.

A survey, on the other hand, is a list of general questions that are asked to a group of people. The answers are then tallied up to help the surveyor come to a conclusion.

Both interviews and surveys are great adds to implement in a book. They both involve outsiders, give fluff to the pages, and they increase readership.

Involving Outsiders- Let's face it; there are many people who feel honored at the thought of having their names mentioned in a book. At the same time, every person interviewed or surveyed will likely sell or buy at least five to ten copies of your book, or more.

Giving Fluff- No author wants a book that looks like a few pieces of paper folded in half. You want your book to be thick enough to have a spine. The thicker the book, the better it looks.

Increasing Readership- As mentioned earlier,

the people interviewed and surveyed will likely sell or buy at least five to ten copies of your book. This increases your audience of readers (if your book is good), and it helps to establish you as an author.

It also increases readership because people often like to buy books that are backed by research and filled with interviews; that's only if the author interviews people who are significant to the book's subject.

There are a variety of ways to conduct interviews and surveys, but here are a few of my favorites:

Interviews

Cyber-Interviews by Email- When I interviewed people for Anointed Fire Magazine, I did not call them, because that would've been too time-consuming; not to mention, I wouldn't have been able to keep up with their words. Because we were in different states, I conducted interviews by email. To do this, you simply type out a list of questions and send them to the person to be interviewed. If the interview will show a dialogue between you and the person being interviewed, be sure to tell them that you will add responses to their responses after they have submitted them. For example, review the line of questioning below:

- **What made you decide to become a singer?**
- **How old were you when you decided that you wanted to make singing a career?**
- **What obstacles have you faced during your transition from a street singer to a worldwide performer?**

Let's assume that the person answers all of the questions this way:

- **What made you decide to become a**

singer?

My Dad used to sing. I adored hearing him sing, and I was especially blessed when I watched the people in the congregation crying as he lifted his voice in worship.

- **How old were you when you decided that you wanted to make singing a career?**

I was 12-years-old when I first decided that I wanted to make a career of singing. It wasn't an easy journey because my Mother wasn't happy about me following in my Father's footsteps; nevertheless, she's a proud Mother now.

- **What obstacles have you faced during your transition from a street singer to a worldwide performer?**

I dealt with rejection; actually, I had to learn to master being rejected. It was hard at first because I allowed people to tell me what they thought I was worth. That was until a man named Trent came along and told me his story. Trent is a well-known gospel singer and I admired him so much. After hearing his story, I was encouraged to press forward.

As you can see, the artist answered the questions; nevertheless, the interviewer now appears to be somewhat rude. Rather than acknowledging what the interviewee has said, the interviewer moved on to the next question. What you would do after you have received the response from the person being interviewed is simply add a response on top of the next question. Review how I revised the line of questioning below to make the interview appear live.

- **What made you decide to become a singer?**
  My Dad used to sing. I adored hearing

him sing, and I was especially blessed when I watched the people in the congregation crying as he lifted his voice in worship.

- **That's awesome. Many artists with the talent to sing inherited that gift from one or both of their parents. How old were you when you decided that you wanted to make singing a career?**

I was 12-years-old when I first decided that I wanted to make a career of singing. It wasn't an easy journey because my Mother wasn't happy about me following in my Father's footsteps; nevertheless, she's a proud Mother now.

- **That's funny because your Mother was married to your Dad and wasn't happy about his decision to sing; therefore, automatically she would be upset about you deciding to sing. I**

know that had to be a pretty big weight, and I know that had to be an obstacle for you at first. What other obstacles have you faced during your transition from a street singer to a worldwide performer?

I dealt with rejection; actually, I had to learn to master being rejected. It was hard at first because I allowed people to tell me what they thought I was worth. That was until a man named Trent came along and told me his story. Trent is a well-known gospel singer and I admired him so much. After hearing his story, I was encouraged to press forward.

- **Wow, that's profound and I think every artist needs to hear your testimony.**

As you can see, I highlighted the extra text added. I did this so that I could send it back to the artist for their approval and give them the opportunity to address anything I said. I also tailored each question based on their response and set it up so that it could flow into the next question.

I won't suggest any other types of interviews for a book except email-to-email, because voice interviews have to be transcribed. If you are interviewing several people, you can choose to ask them the same questions, or you can ask a different set of questions.

Of course there is face-to-face interviewing, but how does this work for a book? It doesn't. Again, voice interviews have to be transcribed; therefore, it is better to do email-to-email so that the person being interviewed can review what they have said, and you can save yourself time.

Note: When conducting an email-to-email interview, make sure the document you send the questions on is professional. If you have a professional letterhead, use it. Be sure to provide a space for the interviewee to answer the questions. Don't just send them a plain word document with questions; otherwise, they may feel that you are unprofessional. Why do their feelings about you matter at this point? Because they are being interviewed. When people feel they are being interviewed by a professional, they assume their interview will be read all around the world. Because of this assumption, they will try to give you a really good interview. If they feel you are unprofessional and the interview will only be read by twelve people, ten of them being your relatives, they won't put too much effort into giving you a good interview. Instead, they will send you quick, short and vague answers to get you off their back.

Surveys are quite different, on the other hand.

Interviews and Surveys

Surveys don't have to be email-to-email. You can conduct surveys on and offline, in person and in private. In addition, surveys don't feature someone in the spotlight; many times, the people who are surveyed are not mentioned when the stats are shown.

Surveys differ somewhat from interviews because they are designed to draw a conclusion. Interviews focus more on the people being interviewed, whereas surveys focus more on the number of people being surveyed as well as their answers.

Surveys can be a list of questions, just like interviews; howbeit, at the end of a survey, you must post the collective results. Surveys are more tedious than interviews, and they take much more time because the results have to be polled.

A great example of a survey is below:

- How many times a day would you say that you talk to GOD?
- Would you say that your prayers to HIM are more positive (praising HIM and thanking HIM) or more needy (asking HIM for something)?
- How often do you attend church services?
- Do you believe in tithes and offering?

Poll Results: Twenty-five (25) of the 50 (or 50%) people surveyed said that they talked with GOD at least twice a day. Ten of the 50 surveyed said they talked with GOD at least once a day, and 15 of the 50 surveyed said they did not talk with GOD on a daily basis.

As you can see from the poll results, you can list it by numbers or by percent. You can also list the people's names or list them as a number. For example, Patricia wants to remain unnamed in the survey; therefore, she is listed as Survey Participant #12. It is always better to have the people sign a disclaimer giving you permission to use their names in the surveys conducted. In surveys, the participants don't have to elaborate on the answers; they simply need to answer the questions that were asked. If you should decide to let them elaborate, you could list what they said throughout your book. It is better to list their elaborations during points where they are actually confirming what you are saying, or you want to challenge what they are saying. Always be sure to let the interviewees know that you may not agree with their answers, but if you disagree, you will be respectful in your response. If they do not want their names listed should you disagree, you will respect their wishes. Also, please note that when listing numbers in surveys, you can list the numerals, no matter how low or high they are. You can also use the percent symbol because people often don't want to read the

Interviews and Surveys

wording. They want to go straight to the numbers.

With surveys, it is also better to list multiple choice answers so that you can easily draw a conclusion based on those answers. Some questions are "yes" and "no" questions; therefore, they are automatically multiple choice; all the same, some questions leave the door open for too many responses. Having too many responses could make it very difficult to draw a conclusion. Judge the questions you ask and determine whether or not they need to be multiple choice, or if you want to leave them open for the survey participants to answer.

At the end of every survey, be sure to poll the results. At the same time, be sure to draw a conclusion from the results, and draw your own conclusion. This helps to engage the reader and opens the door for your next book to be written. Also, be sure to edit the responses from the people who took the survey. Remove any unnecessary wording, jargon or information that does not benefit your poll.

Common First-Time Author Errors

There are certain errors that are common to first-time writers, and they are:

1. **Procrastination.** We all know that this is a setback, but there is something very few people realize about procrastination. When you procrastinate on writing a book, you will oftentimes lose interest in that book as time goes by. When GOD has given you a book to write, HE will stir up your spirit to write it. All too often, would-be authors procrastinate on writing their books because:
   - They don't think they are smart enough.
   - They don't believe they have enough information to write a book.
   - They don't have enough money or

know how to manage their money so they can write the book.

- They don't know where to begin. Another form of procrastination is sitting on a WORD for too long. Some authors have time-lines that they want to complete their books in, but they tend to busy themselves with other chores and put the book last. This is absolute error because information not recorded is often lost, and this causes the author to go under pressure as they attempt to recall the powerful messages they once had. You should never feel pressure when writing, or it'll interrupt your flow.

2. **Trying to sound like other authors.** You are who you are for a reason. Remember, GOD created a unique you for a unique purpose. Anytime an author tries to channel the voice or

writing style of another author, they lose their voice, and their books often flop as a result. As a first-time author, you are still trying to find your writing voice, but this takes time and persistence. You will grow into your writer's voice eventually.

3. **Trying to write about subjects they have no knowledge of.** Let's face it; books written by unknowledgeable authors take too long to write, and they stress the author. It is always better to write what you are passionate and knowledgeable about. A lot of times, you will find authors who can only push one book out a year. That's because many of them have to conduct research on the subject they are writing on. If you find that you are gifted to speak on resolving marriage conflicts, then you should use that gift to write.

4. **Announcing their plans to their friends.** When GOD gives you a book to write, HE only told you for a reason. Sometimes, your friends won't root for you; they'll speak against you. As you mature as a writer, you will find that you will outgrow some of the friendships you once fit in. This is because some people are seasonal and are not meant to come with us to the next level. It is very common for a person once revered as a friend to speak against the author's choice to write, or criticize the author's writings. Let your friends be just as surprised as your audience is.

5. **Ignoring messages from GOD or not being prepared to write down those messages.** Have you ever had a time when GOD said something into your spirit that was so profound that it caught

your attention? You may have been ministering to someone, and wisdom came out of your mouth that you know did not come from your knowledge bank; it had to come from GOD. Nevertheless, when you arrived home, you forgot what you said or how you said it. When GOD says something, write it down! Always be prepared to take notes when GOD speaks.

6. **Not formatting their book properly or trying to do the publisher's job.** As an author, you should separate chapters from chapters, and you must remain consistent throughout your book. If you like to highlight your important messages using bullet points, do so; but be consistent throughout the book. Being inconsistent will often cost you more money, as it will cost the publisher

more time. All the same, when you try to format the book using line breaks and coding, you make the publisher's job harder. Because the publisher's job is harder, your fee will be steeper.

7. **Scriptural errors.** Some authors abbreviate scriptures, and this is wrong. Not everyone knows that Eph. stands for Ephesians. Additionally, some authors are not consistent with the way they write scriptures out. For example, in one section of the book, the author italicizes the scriptures, but in another section, the author places quotations around the scripture. One more scriptural error is trying to write scriptures from memory. This error always ends up costing the writer more money because writers tend to review their books AFTER the editor has

reviewed their books. The editor will often charge more for checking scriptures. The right way to do this is to copy and paste scriptures from an online Bible site.

8. **Using colloquialisms and jargon.** Okay, so the book is getting good (to you), and you want to express how you feel. So, you go throughout the book writing, "Hallelujah! Somebody better give JESUS a crazy praise!" Now, a statement like this is good when you are verbally preaching a message, but you should NEVER incorporate jargon or colloquialisms into your book. Your reader might not be where you are, and such speech will only distract the reader from the book. Always remember to separate your speaking voice from your writing voice.

9. **Prematurely naming your book.** Sure, you may have come up with an awesome name for a book, but this doesn't mean you need to name the book first and then write. Doing so often limits the information you can place in that book. As GOD ministers to you what to write, the information will often bleed over the title. Because of this, many authors end up changing the names of their books again and again. Many end up using the name they'd previously chosen, but they add subtitles to try and cover the new information. You should never do this. You should know what you want to write about first, and then write it. After your book is complete, you can find a title better suited for the book.

10. **Inappropriate use of words.** Some

people use words the wrong way. Always be sure to look in your dictionary before using a word that you are unsure of. Words are like artistic photos. Sometimes, they are beautiful and expressive; other times, they are unappealing and pointless. If you are not sure of the definition of a word, look it up! In addition, if you are not sure what a particular adage or idiom means, look it up before using it.

11. **Writing books that you were not graced to write.** Sure, it sounds like a great idea, but did GOD really tell you to write that book? A lot of authors hear someone else talking about an idea for a book, and they try to run off with it. As a result, many end up writing books they weren't graced to write, and no one buys the book except for a few family

members and friends. Sure, you may have a lot of powerful pointers to add to a book, but it doesn't mean you are supposed to write that book. A few powerful points in a powerless book is draining.

12. **Using lengthy sentences.** This is a headache to a reader who just wants to get to the point. Review the sentence example below. "Martha went to the store and saw Bill buying chicken, and Martha wanted some chicken, so she asked Bill if she could come by his house later to eat some of the chicken, but Bill suspected that Martha was interested in him, so he created an excuse and left the store before Martha could respond." Believe it or not, sentences such as the above one are **very** common with first-time writers.

Common First-Time Author Errors

Remember this rule of thumb: If you have to use the conjunctive words "and", "but" or "so" more than three times, the sentence is too long. I recommend only using a conjunction two times in a sentence. Another common lenghty sentence example is: "The greatest achievement one can witness in their lives is the fulfillment of their purpose, winning souls for CHRIST and helping others to achieve their purpose in such a wicked, thoughtless and cruel world that swallows people whole and spits them out." As you can see, the above sentence is almost a paragraph long. Needless to say, the sentence could be broken down into two sentences. The subject of a sentence should not change mid-sentence. Instead, when we spoke of the "greatest achievement," we should have stayed there. When we decided to speak about this cruel world, we should have created a new sentence; or better yet, a new paragraph.

13. **Writing too much about self.** If you are not writing a biography, the only time you should mention yourself is when you are giving a personal testimony. A testimony is great but should only be given to explain your point; it should not be an off-topic discussion. Readers tend to get sucked into what they are reading, and when you're all over the place, they can't really settle down to read your book. Instead, every time you jump from guiding them to pointing back at yourself, you are acting as a bookmark. You want to draw them into the book, not into you.

14. **Using "this" or "that" should be done to continue a statement.** Always be sure that the readers understand what "this" and "that" means to your sentence. It is better to just reiterate who or what you are talking about specifically than to confuse the reader. An example is: "Patricia woke Terry up to ask him about the excessive calls to a 414 number that she'd seen on the bill. Terry was dazed, but he didn't want to talk about that. He began to look at the phone bill, and he recognized who the number belonged to, and that upset him. He immediately turned to Patricia and told her that he was tired of her insecurities and that was the number to his sister in Wisconsin. That made Patricia feel awful since she'd done that." As you can see, the readers have their work cut out for them. They have

to reread the sentences to figure out who or what "that" is. Readers like to flow. The correct way to have written the above paragraph is as follows: "Patricia woke Terry up to ask him about the excessive calls to a 414 number ~~that~~ she'd seen on the bill. Terry was dazed, but he didn't want to talk about ~~that~~ the phone bill at the moment. As he began to look at the document, he recognized who the number belonged to, ~~and that upset him~~ and he became upset. He immediately turned to Patricia and told her that he was tired of her insecurities. ~~and that was t~~ The number belonged to his sister in Wisconsin. ~~That made~~ Hearing Terry's response made Patricia feel awful. ~~since she'd done that.~~" I struck through the unnecessary words so the readers could get to the facts of the story without having to go through excessive words.

15. **Going from first person to third person.** First person examples include: I, me and we. Second person includes: You and yours. Third person includes: He, she, their or they. If you are writing a book in first person, you must continue to write it that way. If you are writing in third person, continue to write in third person. An example of an awful read is as follows: "Once upon a time there lived a man named Tron. Tron was an exceptional man who loved to dance, and he loved to sing. I got my singing capabilities from my dad. He used to sing solos at our local church, and I admired his voice. People often noticed that Tron would mimic his dad's key, but he also had his own unique sound." As

Common First-Time Author Errors

you can see from the sentence, the reader has no choice but to be confused. First, we are speaking of Tron in third person. Then, we went into speaking as Tron. This is a no-no in writing. Find your position and stay there.

Overcoming Writer's Block

Oftentimes, you will find yourself sitting at a computer with the desire to write but not a writer's thought in sight. You may find yourself sitting there for hours at a time and becoming even more frustrated as time flies by. All you have are a few lines on a document. Here are a few tips to overcoming Writer's Block....from a Christian perspective.

1. **Change your room around, or change rooms.** Sometimes, certain environments are too distracting and may actually work more against you than they work for you. If the room is dirty, clean it up. If the room is cluttered, find an uncluttered room or get up and organize the room. Just make sure that the room you are in is peaceful. If you

can't find a peaceful room in your house, you may be able to find peace at some local cafes with internet access.

2. **Turn off the television.** Your mind will never allow you to focus when there is something or someone else in the room attempting to communicate with you.

3. **Make your favorite shows tune into you.** Writers are often made to break habits in order to write.

4. **Understand that most authors have pitbull tenacity.** Don't lock into something that is not benefiting you. Online video games and certain television shows may be fun, but are they beneficial? Remember this: Video game players get better at playing games; television watchers get better at

watching, but those who forsake idleness to walk in their GOD-given roles get better at being busy. Some people will walk in their success, while others will sit back and watch.

5. **Work when everyone is asleep or at work/school.** As a writer, you will often find that your thoughts will flow freely when there are no people around to engage them. Even quiet people can be distracting to writers, because we tend to worry about the needs of our loved ones above our own needs.

6. **Research and research some more!** It's okay to read someone else's article to stir up your mind. Of course, you should never steal their information; but oftentimes, we come into that infamous writer's block. Reading an article will

often help you to re-engage your mind, and you will find that many times the author may list a pointer that you have absolutely forgotten. All the same, one pointer from another author may wake up five pointers and ideas in you. Just remember, do not steal anyone's text or information. Just treat the reading as if you and that person were having a conversation.

7. **Go and do everything else you need to do first...and then come back to writing.** As a writer, you will find that any little thing can be distracting to you. Maybe you need to wash the dishes, but you want to write a few pages before you start; nevertheless, you can't seem to write because those dishes are there. It is better to get up and do what you need to do first, so that you can get

back to writing without having other things playing tug-of-war with your mind.

8. Settle any feuds or disagreements you may have in your home. Satan has two weapons he likes to use on Christian authors: One is pride, and the other is fear. GOD resists the proud, and Satan knows this; therefore, if you are operating in pride, you won't hear from GOD. You may find that the people around you will often step on your toes when you are preparing to write. Instead of getting angry, make a conscious decision to forgive them and do something positive with them or for them. Secondly, don't let fear come your way. Fear opposes faith, and fear also stands between GOD'S voice and you. You may fear sounding a certain way, and this is normal; especially if this is your first book. But no worries. Most first-time authors have that fear, and many of them get over the fear to write some pretty powerful best-sellers.

9. **When you're broken, you need to grab your notepad and write!** GOD speaks clearly to a broken spirit. If you're going through a storm, now is not the time to take a break. Quite the contrary. When you're going through a storm, you need to open up your notebook and write. Don't write on your computer; write in your notebook whatever GOD tells you to write. Ask HIM for the wisdom in the situation and write it down. Don't write in your actual book at this time, because some people write from the flesh when they are upset. Nevertheless, if you have submitted yourself to GOD, you are like

a conduit that GOD can speak through. When you are calm again, reread what you have written and transfer the wisdom from your notes into your book. Be sure to throw away the fleshy stuff that may be hanging off of it.

10. Don't eat a heavy meal before writing.

Heavy meals tend to weigh us down and make us want to take a nap. The mind's activity will slow down when you begin to get sleepy. It is better to eat fruit, nuts, berries and drink plenty of water. This snack is light, and it'll often energize you.

11. Coffee is not always the answer.

Coffee energizes the body, but not the mind; so you may want to stay away from coffee and any other caffeine-filled products. All the same, coffee users often crash. Crashing is a term used to describe the heaviness a person feels after the caffeine has worn off.

12. **Exercise actually stimulates the mind.** Get up and do a quick ten-minute workout to get your mind pumped. Sometimes, you may find yourself feeling tired as you write. This is a great time to stand up and get a little workout in. This will often reengage the mind to write; all the same, it helps you to get and stay in shape.

13. **Don't force it!** It's okay to take a break when your body and mind are requesting one. Just know the difference between taking a break and procrastinating. Don't give in to the flesh to procrastinate. If you're frustrated, your book will sound like

you're frustrated. Step back and dose up on some happiness before starting again.

14. **Turn off your cell phone if you can.** It only takes one ring of the phone to stop that flow you had going. If you have children who are not at home, I wouldn't recommend turning off the phone. If your children are at home with you, turning off your phone may mean the difference in taking one year to complete your book as opposed to five weeks.

15. **Talk on the phone when you need a break.** Sometimes you will find that discussing what you are writing about will give you some ideas for new content. Call a person you can discuss the information with and talk about it. Don't tell them you are writing a book or

trying to get stirred up. Instead, just bring up the conversation randomly and naturally let it flow.

16. **Step away from the computer and grab your notepad.** Sometimes a computer can be overwhelming. Simply take your notepad to a quiet room and just write down some pointers. The pointers should help you to flow when you're ready to get back to the computer. Oftentimes, your mind will re-energize when you go away from the computer. Don't write your book in the notepad, however. Instead, think of some pointers, sentences and chapter headings to add to your book.

17. **Interview people.** Find people who can relate to or testify about the subject you are writing on and interview them. You

can also conduct surveys to get more information. Interviews are a super-source of information, and they provide you with extra content for your book.

18. **Use the people you know as templates.** People around writers quickly learn that they are used as templates pretty often as they witness certain stories and advice that seem to hit home for them. All the same, writers don't always intentionally write about the people they know; sometimes we do it subconsciously because we are recorders of information. We take lessons and store them away for creative times. Anytime you find yourself in writer's block, ask yourself which character you know that can benefit from your book. Then start advising them via your book. In doing

so, you will advise many who are like them.

19. Pray about it. This is obvious; right? Sometimes there are things, people and situations that are keeping us from hearing from GOD. Oftentimes, it's not writer's block that we are trying to get past; it's a block from hearing GOD'S voice. Humble yourself and ask the LORD to remove this block.

20. Take a day off from time to time, but not often. Let's face it; some days will come that we won't be able to write the way we want to. Take the day off to recharge, but don't let yourself be idle that day. Study and conduct research instead.

21. Facebook it. What area are you having

the block in? What were you writing about? Ask a question on Facebook and see if any of the answers can help to drive you through that block. Don't tell anyone that you are writing a book on the subject. Instead, ask a question and see what people are saying. You can even inbox some of your friends and ask them to share their feedback on your status. You can tell them you are writing a book if you choose to, but be sure to tell them that their answers won't be published in your book; you are simply using their answers to pull you out of a block. Personally, I wouldn't tell anyone what I was writing about, because this often stirs up other authors. Believe it or not, many authors will try to write a book similar to yours if they know you are in the process of writing it. Needless to say, they don't often do this when your book is published because they don't want to be seen as a copycat.

22. Put down that other author's book! A book written by someone else can actually be the enemy of a writer who is trying to add text to their own book. This depends on the author, however. Books written by other authors can be intimidating for most first-time authors. Other people's info tends to seem more powerful than your input because your input is familiar to you, whereas theirs is not. Some authors may have an opposite reaction...but it's okay to test yourself and see if you do well with other books. We mentioned reading articles earlier, but articles are subject related, and you can get directly to the point, whereas books take you on a long journey before you can get to the information you were looking for. While this may help you to come out of your writer's block, it will often work against you. How so? Information that you were initially going to share will be lost as you witness another author sharing info similar to or contradictory of what you wanted to share. It may cause you to question your book or feel as if you are stealing their information. When I am writing a book on a particular subject, I absolutely refuse to read anyone else's book on that subject until I've published my book. It's okay to scan through a book to help yourself get out of writer's block, but to read another author's book during your writing time can often work against you.

23. Get negative people out of your ear,

and stop letting people read what you have written so far. People who are familiar with us won't always give us an A+ with our writing assignments because they are familiar with us. It's hard for someone who has intimate access to you to view you as a best-seller or as a professional. Instead, to them you are just you. Familiar people will often grade you well but discourage you by asking menacing questions like, "Why did you write it this way? What point are you trying to get at here? I'm not understanding." Remember that they are familiar with you and see you in an intimate light. Everyone has their "writer's" voice, and others will try to impose their "writer's voice" upon you.

24. **Go ahead and pay for your publishing.** This is a great way to make

it "real" to you. Oftentimes, the whole idea of becoming an author seems like a race we are running, and we simply hope that we'll cross the finished line. Most first-time authors see their potential books the same way they see a million dollars: it seems like a dream so far away that they can't reach it just yet. But you need to make it real to *you*, if nothing else. To do this, go ahead and find your publisher...and then pay them for the publishing. This is a great way to put "fire under your hiney" and make you go ahead and write that book.

25. **Remember...writer's block may also be GOD saying you are going in the wrong direction with your writing.** Repent and get back on course. You should know already where HE has called you to be....whether you want to

be there or not. Don't deviate from the message that GOD is giving you; otherwise, you may end up writing the book without HIM.

Finding the Right Words

How often are you challenged by words? As a writer, you will find that the right words will seem to escape you when you need them the most. Then again, your vocabulary is limited to words you are familiar with, and this is oftentimes not enough for the average writer. After all, we often read books where the authors are using words that we can't even pronounce, let alone define. For this very reason, many would-be authors reject their gifts of writing. There are a few things you need to understand, and they are:

1. **You are not them (other writers), and they are not you.** You can't sound like them, and they can't sound like you. Anytime an author tries to channel the voice of another author, their books flop. That's because human beings have a

gift for detecting phony. Anytime I edit books, I can tell when I am reading the author's voice or a character voice that they have adopted. The author's voice often reads authentic and is very inviting despite their limitations; howbeit, the character voice seems staged. Have you ever watched a commercial where the person was loud and obviously reading from a script? That's what the wrong voice reads like. It sounds scripted and fake.

2. **You can never find your voice if you are using someone else's.** Writers usually start off iffy, but as time goes on, they mature in their gifting. As you mature, writing will become a second nature to you. It'll be fun, and you'll love the freedom of being who you are. At the same time, your audience will love

the opportunity to get to know you through your writings.

3. **If you can't pronounce it, don't write it!** How embarrassing it is to come across a person who has read and enjoyed one of your books, and they bring up a specific line that tickled or shocked them. And then they do it....they ask you to repeat that line because they want to hear you say it. Now you're over there stuttering and stumbling over your own words. Be yourself; people will love you and need to love you as such.

4. **The right words are just a Google search away.** Some people like to whip out the old hard back dictionary or thesaurus trying to find the right words, but a Google search can pull it up a lot

faster and give you more options. Search for words, study them, and use them. Writers shop for words because we need as many of them as we can get!

5. **Your words should represent your personality.** If you know you don't use words like expenditure, conglomerate, perspicacious, recapitalization; don't write them. When you have author signings, many of the people who buy your book will speak with you. If you don't sound like the same person in the book, they will likely never buy from you again. Remember, when you sell one book, you are selling future books. One book never just sells itself. You are also selling yourself as a writer, and even if you get better over time; people who were victims of your "bad era" will have

trouble forgiving and trusting you with their time and money again.

6. **Remember to consider your audience.** Every book has an audience, and you need to know who your book's audience is. Who is likely to buy your book? Don't say everyone, because this is never the case. You may write it for everyone, but you have to consider that a certain age group, gender and race is more likely to buy your books than others. Knowing your target market will determine whether you become a best-selling author or just another author. With that said, don't write a book for a twenty to thirty-year-old audience using words fit for a 12-year-old. All the same, don't use hip words on an audience of thirty plus. Your readers will get lost somewhere in

the words and the frustration.

7. **It's okay to delete whole sentences and even whole pages!** As a writer, there will come a time where you'll open up a document you've been writing in. You'll reread it and discover you hate the way it sounds. The choice of words, the babbling and the run-on sentences will be too much if you should run into them. Then comes the challenge. You've got paragraphs or pages of nonsense, but you don't want to lose all of that text. After all, you've put in a lot of work writing it. It is better to lose the text than to lose the reader. Now if you can rewrite the text and make it read better, then do so. Open up a second document and try to revise it until it sounds right. Then paste it over the original text. But if it just makes no

Finding the Right Words

sense and has no place, don't force it there. Put it out of its misery before your readers end up paying good money for a bad read. Please know that one paragraph can ruin an entire book.

But how do you find the right words for you? It's simple. Use the words you ordinarily use. It's okay to add new words; words you can pronounce and incorporate into your vocabulary. As a matter of fact, it is good, as a writer, to learn at least one new word a day.

Below are some sites you will find helpful.

www.thesaurus.com
www.synonym.com
www.merriam-webster.com
www.thefreedictionary.com
www.dictionary.reference.com

Writing Strategies

Every author should have strategies to help them over the course of their writing. Every book that you write is like a building being put together. Every sentence is like a brick, and every word is like the mortar that makes it all stick together. When writing, always remember that you are building. Readers who buy your books are actually visiting the content of your hearts. If the content is good, they are happy; nevertheless, how you present the content will determine whether they want to visit your world anymore.

Below are a few writing strategies:

1. **What fascinates you the most?**
   People tend to talk non-stop about the things that fascinate them. A woman

fascinated by make-up will often become talkative when the subject of cosmetics is brought up. A man who is fascinated with body building may go on for hours showing off his weight-loss, fitness knowledge and his biceps. That's because we are passionate about whatever we are knowledgeable about. Therefore, write about what fascinates you, and from there, you will flow like a river.

2. **Relate your stories to your testimonies.** Testimonies are great to give when you aren't soaking the reader in yourself. What this means is that you are not putting too many topics about you in the book...unless the book relates to you. People like a good laugh. Tell them your funny stories, but make sure there is a message behind those stories,

and make sure that the message directly relates to what you are writing about. Readers love testimonies; make sure they are pointed and not pointless.

3. **Again, conduct interviews with people.** This is a great way to add pages and depth to your book. Having the testimonies of at least ten men or women in the book will prove to be beneficial for the reader and yourself.

4. **There is often a certain room in the house, or a certain spot that you find yourself thinking the most.** Take your laptop or notebook and head to that spot. If it's not at home, make sure it's in a safe place where you'll be able to concentrate.

5. **Help your accountability partner.** You

will find that when you help someone else, the ideas will often start to flow in your own mind. Therefore, it's a good idea to email or call the partner from time to time and ask if they need help.

6. **Watch a movie with a subject line that relates to what you are writing.** For example, if you are writing a book about marriage and how to stay married, you should watch a movie that details the struggles of marriage. Then imagine yourself counseling each individual involved. As you counsel them mentally, you will often find ideas flowing through your mind at alarming rates. Pause the movie to address the situation the actor is in, making sure to record your notes as you go along.

7. **Think about someone you know who**

your advice could help, and then write the book as if you are writing them a note. Don't be afraid to tell them the truth...just let GOD flow in and through you.

8. **Visit www.amazon.com and search for books related to what you are writing about.** Many of Amazon's books have a feature called "Look Inside." Open up some of the books and read. Do not for any reason steal the author's information. The purpose of opening the book is to stir up some ideas in you. As you read, you may find yourself agreeing with the author and wanting to further elaborate on the issue, or disagreeing with the author and give correcting information about the issue. Don't read the entire book. Just read a few lines to stir you up.

9. **Fast and write.** The greatest voice you can hear is directly from GOD HIMSELF. Sometimes, a fast is what we need to tear down any walls that are standing between us and the LORD.

10. **Print what you have written and read it.** This will often help you once you are away from your computer, and you can see your book in another light....literally. Be sure to edit as you go along. That way, you don't end up paying excessive fees to your hired editor. After printing the book, go into another room to edit it.

11. **Change your clothes.** This may be weird and definitely unconventional, but oftentimes we try to write in clothes that are uncomfortable to us. We may not recognize how uncomfortable those clothes are until we are truly ready to

relax. Get comfortable and then start writing. In doing so, you will help your mind to relax, and a relaxed mind is free to flow.

Obstacles and Errors

In writing, you will come across a few obstacles that will threaten the life or impact of your book. These obstacles include, but are not limited to the following:

Fear- Most Christian authors hold back on preaching what the LORD taught them because they fear being wrong or they fear backlash from people. Some messages given to us by GOD are so deep that the average author either tries to water it down or refuses to publish it at all. At the same time, many authors know people who are in the situations they are writing about, and they fear these people may feel the book was tailored just to them. Therefore, authors tend to edit and re-edit what they wrote, removing the power from their books one sentence at a time.

Obstacles and Errors

Self- Many authors put too much of themselves in the book. While your readers will find reading about you interesting when what you are writing about lines up with your testimony, too much of you can turn the reader off. If it's a self-help book, it needs to help, and you can testify along the way. If it's a fictional book, it needs to be just that: fictional. You can also change the names of the characters and put them in situations you've been in.

Self-Righteous Tones- Many Christian writers unknowingly write with a self-righteous tone. While it is good to be confident, your tone should never be read as "I've got this Christian thing down pat, and now I need to school you." Your readers need to see your struggle from defeat to victory...and then from victory to victory again. Readers need to be able to relate to you and what you are writing.

Condemning "You" - Oftentimes, Christian authors speak on certain types of behaviors and spirits, and this is good. But the problem that arises is they speak as if they are speaking to the reader. Using the term "you" or any personal term when delivering a rebuke is never a good idea. The proper way is to make the reader believe you are together against a mindset or a spirit, or that you are trying to help them get delivered from a mindset or a spirit. They should never feel attacked when reading your book.

Problem Example: The spirit of hatred is so widespread in the church! Why do you hate others? Why do you think GOD doesn't see your iniquities? Soon, you will reap what you have sown!

Proper Example: The spirit of hatred is so widespread in the church! Why do some people hate others? Why do they think GOD doesn't see their iniquities? We all know they shall reap what they have sown!

As you can see, in the "Problem Example", the writer comes off as bitter, and their book reads like an angry note to whomever they are speaking against. In the "Proper Example", the writer comes off as knowledgeable, and their book reads like a concerned person who has witnessed an issue in the church and wants to correct it. Even if the reader is guilty of the sin you are teaching against, he won't feel attacked; he'll feel rebuked. There is a big difference!

Reverence of Man- Some authors go throughout their books talking about other authors or men and women of GOD. It's okay to refer to another person, their deeds and what they have said. But you shouldn't make the majority or half of your book point outward. Instead, share the knowledge GOD has given you so the readers will want to come back and buy your next book; otherwise, they'll simply go and look for the river they believe you are sourcing from.

Too Many Exclamation Points- I know you want to express how intense you believe that last sentence is, but you have to leave it up to the reader to decide how powerful it is to them. It's just like the Bible; there are some scriptural references that are powerful to some people who were granted revelation; whereas, to others, the scripture appears to be a group of words that don't make sense. Try not to use too many exclamation points in your book. As a matter of fact, use them scarcely. At the same time, use one exclamation point when making an expressive statement; try not to use four and five exclamation points at a time.

Friendly Discouragement- Let's face it:

Obstacles and Errors

Some people who are familiar with us can never truly see us as authors. It doesn't matter how long you've been in ministry; there are some people who know you by the flesh, and they just can't dine at your table. Many authors send their books to these characters to be judged, and the person judges their flesh and not the content of the book. All the same, some people brandish their envious fangs when they see you stepping up into a new title. This even happens after the book is published and selling. You'll often hear from friends and family members who want you to know they have just purchased your book and it was "okay" to them. Their goal is to discourage you, and this often works when they point out errors they've found or they question the choice of words you used. Don't be discouraged. The quickest way to run these types away is to start praising GOD in their ears for the people who have given you a great report on the book.

Seeking Man's Approval- A lot of authors go through a faith struggle while they are writing. Even though they believe GOD told them to write something, they worry that it'll scare people, anger people or offend people. So what they do is go to another person and ask for that person's opinion. If that person has not received revelation from GOD, they will never give a good review to you. This can be and almost always is discouraging.

Uncertain Tones- Many new authors are afraid to write in confidence; therefore, they write in a way that sounds as if they are uncertain about what they are writing. This is a turn off for most readers, and it opens the door for arrogant or platform-seeking readers to object and correct.

Problem Example: I once heard someone say

that many diseases aren't rooted in the flesh; they've simply come to show you what's going on in your spirit. I'm not sure, but their point was interesting.

Proper Example: I once heard someone say that many diseases aren't rooted in the flesh; they've simply come to show you what's going on in your spirit. This is so true!

Remember, your readers are looking for answers; they aren't looking for authors who don't have them.

Writing Poorly and Thinking the Editor Will Fix It- Editors rank books according to the amount of work that has to be done in them. If you submit a poorly written book, you may end up paying up to four times more money than someone who took the time to correct themselves and clean up their books.

Book Professionalism

When writing a book, you will find that the text will often go in a different direction than the direction you planned for it to go. That's because we have plans, but our plans aren't always GOD'S plans. Because of this divide, we often sacrifice professionalism trying to mix what GOD told us to write with what we want to write. This often leads to powerless books with powerful pointers scattered throughout them.

When writing your book, you must remain professional with your writing to ensure that you don't limit your book to a specific audience. This isn't easy at first because, as new writers, you are still trying to find your footing. Here are 11 things you should know and do to keep your book professional:

1. **Avoid using too much wit.** You may find that you are a witty person, and people often laugh at your spunky words and attitude, but your attitude won't carry over well on paper. Instead of using wit, be yourself but in a professional way. Don't try to sell yourself as a funny character; sell your words because that's what the readers will read.

2. **Avoid using slang and broken English.** Within our own crowds, our way of talking is accepted, and we oftentimes don't care what anyone thinks of us who are outside of our crowds. Using improper English is only good if you are writing to a particular crowd; nevertheless, if you are targeting a larger group of people, you've just assassinated your book's potential.

Slang and broken English may go over in a theater as a play, but it will never read well in a book unless you are targeting an audience of slang speakers.

3. **Each sentence should lead you to the next sentence.** Words are like ushers; they take you to a place where you can relax or shout. All the same, each paragraph should prepare the reader for the next paragraph. Please understand that changing subjects or characters mid-sentence often comes off as a poorly inserted commercial. Oftentimes, your readers will be planning to read just a few pages of your book, and then they intend to get back to what they've planned. When a book is good, they'll lose track of the time and continue the book until their curiosity or their hunger

for wisdom has been satisfied. But if you insert off-subject pointers mid-sentence, you are acting as a bookmark in your own book.

4. **Never go on and on about a point you've already made.** Your readers want to move to the next point as fast as they can. Sometimes you will find that a particular pointer is good to you, and you may want to elaborate on it. Elaborating on a point is okay if you go ahead and do it when you make the initial statement, or if you do so within the next few paragraphs. But if you lead your readers to one place and then take them back to a place they've already been, you will only confuse and irritate them.

5. **Your book's cover design should**

speak to the content of your book. Never try to design a cover yourself, and never hire someone who isn't a professional. Your book's cover will sell more than fifty percent of your books, as it is the face of your book; it is your content's visual representative.

6. **Avoid do-it-yourself options unless you are a professional.** All too often, authors try to save themselves money by trying to publish their books themselves, or they have someone do it for them as a favor. The people they give their books to are often not professional publishers; therefore, the book ends up put together poorly. Pages have to be setup properly to sell books.

7. **You're an okay editor; understand**

that and hire a professional editor. Most people who are pretty good writers believe they are good enough to personally edit their own books. To save themselves a few hundred or thousand dollars, they reread their own books several times to look for errors. After that, they send the book to be published. Once the book is published and available for the whole world to see, they go back and review the book from an objective point of view. What they find are errors logged upon errors. They then contact the publisher requesting the book be taken down so they can make some adjustments. Of course, in doing this, the publisher is going to charge the author more money because they were hired to publish the book...not publish and unpublish it over and over again. A publisher charges for the work, but mostly for the time spent preparing and completing the work.

8. **Don't consider your book dimensions; let your book's page count determine what dimensions are best for you.** All too often, an author settles their mind on what size their books are going to be, but they don't write enough pages to make the book look professional. If you are planning to print your book, you need to understand that the amount of pages in your book will determine whether or not your book has a spine. For example, let's consider an author writes a forty-page book (8x11), and wants to publish it as a 6x9. This would mean that the author's book will likely have 55-60 pages, and the book's spine will be too thin to hold any text. After the author receives their

book, they are regretful and request that the publisher republish the book as a 5x8. Of course, the publisher will oftentimes charge the author one hundred percent of the publishing price again because they are having to reformat and republish the book. If your book doesn't have at least 120 pages as an 8x11 document, you should publish it as a 5x8 or at least a 5.5 x 8.5. The smaller the page count, the thinner the spine will be, but if you'd like to get a decent sized spine, you should go with a 5x8.

9. **Always use basic or readable fonts.** Fonts like Comic Sans should not be used in a book. Of course, this is always up to the author, but in most cases where the font is used, the author changes his or her mind and wants to

go with a basic font once they see the book in print. Again, this ends up costing the author more money with the publisher because the book has to be reformatted with the new font. If you'd like to test a font out, first change the font on one page of your book. After that, you can simply highlight that particular page of your book and print it. If you like the font, go with it. Don't use cursive or fancy fonts unless you are using them in the header, and they are readable. Remember, once the book goes to the publisher, you're stuck with whatever you send UNLESS you pay a re-publish fee. The best fonts to use for books are basic fonts.

10. **Always avoid using too much text on your book's cover.** Ask your book cover designer what is best for the cover

of your book, and consider what they share with you. Many first-time authors think they'll sell more units of their books if they added more pointers to the front cover of the book, and this is not true. Your book cover should be a design, the title, subtitle, author's name, and you can even add a few pointers if needed.

11. **Don't try to show all of your different personality degrees in one book.** It is great to be versatile, but you don't want to come off as being all over the place. Save some of that versatility for other books to come so that you can broaden your audience.

12. **When copying and pasting text from another source, always copy and paste the text into Notepad first.** Many sites such as online Bible sites

and online dictionaries incorporate coding and links into their text. When you copy and paste their text directly into a word document, you will often see underlined words highlighted in blue. This means there is coding there, and if someone were to purchase the e-book, they would be able to click those links and go to the site that you took the text from. Pasting the text into Notepad removes the coding. You simply paste it there, highlight it, copy it and transfer it to the word document you are using to write your book. With scriptures, always remember to remove the numbers that precede the scriptures UNLESS you are listing the scriptures in a row.

Wrong Way: "**1**As a prisoner for the Lord, then, I urge you to live a life worthy of the calling you have received. **2**Be completely humble and gentle; be patient, bearing with one another in love. **3**Make every effort to keep the unity of the Spirit through the bond of peace. **4**There is one body and one Spirit, just as you were called to one hope when you were called; **5**one Lord, one faith, one baptism; **6**one God and Father of all, who is over all and through all and in all. **7**But to each one of us grace has been given as Christ apportioned it" (Ephesians 4:1-7).

As you can see, the numbers make it hard to read the text, and if you are reading this book in e-book format, you will notice that by mousing over the numbers, the website www.biblehub.com shows up.

Right Way: "As a prisoner for the Lord, then, I urge you to live a life worthy of the calling you have received. Be completely humble and gentle; be patient, bearing with one another in love. Make every effort to keep the unity of the Spirit through the bond of peace. There is one body and one Spirit, just as you were called to one hope when you were called; one Lord, one faith, one baptism; one God and Father of all, who is over all and through all and in all. But to each one of us grace has been given as Christ apportioned it" (Ephesians 4:1-7).

Another Right Way:

1. As a prisoner for the Lord, then, I urge you to live a life worthy of the calling you have received.

2. Be completely humble and gentle; be patient, bearing with one another in love.

3. Make every effort to keep the unity of the Spirit through the bond of peace.

4. There is one body and one Spirit, just as you were called to one hope when you were called;

5. one Lord, one faith, one baptism;

6. one God and Father of all, who is over all and through all and in all.

7. But to each one of us grace has been given as Christ apportioned it.

Book Professionalism

It is very unprofessional to list links, tables and text that have not had the links removed from them.

Locating Your Target Audience

As an author, it is absolutely vital to your book's existence that you locate your target audience. Let's be real here; your book is not going to be the hot topic of every age group, gender, race or religion. Every author has a hot market, but only those who identify their markets actually sell books. The rest end up marketing amiss, as they continue to advertise their books to people who are simply not interested.

If you ever find yourself in a spot where people just aren't buying your books, you are likely marketing to the wrong group of people. As an author, you are not to find success; you are simply to find your target audience, and you'll find that success was waiting there for you all along. At the same time, you should always consider broadening your audience while you write. Sometimes authors limit their audience to their peers, and while this is okay, their books don't sell many units. When I say "peers", I don't just mean people of their age groups; many authors limit themselves to a certain group of people. For example, some books by African American authors tend to be geared more at other African Americans. If this is what you want, then it's okay. But if you are looking for a diverse crowd, you must learn to write in a manner that is understood by all groups.

Ask yourself the following questions to help you determine who your target audience is:
1. What age group is most likely to be interested in my book?
2. What gender is most likely to be interested in my book?

3. What race is most likely to be interested in my book?
4. What is the income bracket of the people who are most likely to be interested in my book?
5. What is the education level of the people who are most likely to be interested in my book?

To find the answer to the questions, sometimes you have to ask yourself, "Exactly how will my book affect the lives of people?" This question alone helps you to visualize who is likely to use your book as a guide to help them get out of a situation they don't want to be in, or to get into a situation they want to be in. For example, a book about failing relationships won't do so well with a fifty year-old woman because most women in that age range are settled into marriages, or settled into their single life. Young women between the ages of 18-35 are more likely to buy books about relationships than any other age group. Biographies are likely to sell more to your peers. Again, when I say peers, I don't just mean your age group, but people who are more like you and can relate more to you. Books about entrepreneurship are more likely to sell to the thirty and over crowd.

How to Make Money Selling Your Books

Let's face it. People don't just write books to see their names in print. We write books for several reasons. As Christian authors, we often write because it is what GOD told us to do. We talk to a few people and learn that we have been granted the key of knowledge in certain areas, and we want to share that knowledge with others. The blessing on the other side of this rainbow is the fact that we are getting paid to share what we know.

People who accuse authors of being money grubbing are very misinformed. Writing a book actually costs money, and many authors never earn the money back that they have spent paying for editing, publishing, cover design and distribution. Yet, the majority of authors who have been given the gift of writing continue to write because it's not all about the money; it's about sharing the wealth of knowledge that GOD has given them.

But let's say that you are an author with one hundred books in you. You need to earn to continue to write and publish books. How can you earn money selling your first book and the books to come?

Here are some tips to help you get out there:

1. **Schedule conference calls on the subject your book is about**- Don't tell people that the conference call is to promote your book; otherwise, they won't come on. Instead, whatever subject your book is teaching on, have a conference call about that subject. Invite

around one hundred people onto the conference call. Out of one hundred, 20-50 are likely to come on. Speak on the subject, and answer any questions that the callers may have. At the end of the call, send them to your website, or tell them about your book. Always remember, only ten to twenty percent of the people who say they will buy will actually follow through with purchasing the book. The others will not.

2. **Contact local radio stations and some Internet Radio links such as BlogTalkRadio**- People listen to the radio; we all know that. But what many authors don't know is that radio marketing is a goldmine if you promote your book on stations where your target audience often tunes in. If it's a Christian book, promote it on a Christian

radio station. You can also Google Christian radio hosts on Internet stations and ask them if they'd be willing to interview you. The more, the better.

3. **Rent booths in book fairs and other Christian events in your area**- You can visit your local Chamber of Commerce to get a list of events that will be occurring in your area. Contact the hosts of the events you are interested in to see if you can rent a booth. You can even host events yourself and invite others to attend.

4. **Get book reviews. Remember the tenacious ten.** The tenacious ten are the people who will actually review your book. It is better to give away ten to one hundred copies of your book in exchange for reviews, but remember

only ten to twenty percent of those who promise to review your book will do so. Most people simply want the freebie, but if you know what to expect, you won't be so angered when and if you don't get the amount of reviews you set out to get. Book reviews actually sell books because people don't like to buy anything they believe others may not want.

5. **Set up book signings in your local Christian book store, mall or wherever people frequent**- Make sure these areas are places your target audience frequent so you won't be marketing amiss. Also be sure to ask the store what day is their busiest so you won't end up in there on their slowest day.

6. **Print flyers about your book and leave stacks of them in some of the local businesses.** This is a great marketing ploy that will surely get you a few bites. Go into some local businesses and ask if you could leave your flyers there. Make sure your book's information is on there, along with a synopsis about the book. Always leave around fifty flyers in each establishment. You can also give them to some teenagers and ask them to pass them out at local events.

7. **Promote the characters in your book (if the book is fictitious), and not the book itself**- People will want to know about the character and their struggle, not so much about the book. If you are promoting a fictional book, it is always better to tell readers about the book, but

more so about the characters in the book. They need to feel that the characters are people they'd like to get to know better. Telling them too much about you as an author will either sell you or turn your readers off.

8. **Get a website and sell your books for less than you sell them on sites such as Amazon**- As an author, it is always good to have a website where you can promote your book and any other service or gift you have. Don't settle for low-budget looking websites that serve as distractions. Instead, invest in a nice website where your readers will feel that you are someone they want to know, as opposed to seeing you as someone who wants to be known.

9. **Take to social networks, but inbox**

some of those in your target audience- People on social media will often promise to buy your books, but they won't always come through. Post up on Facebook and Twitter about your book, but also create email campaigns to promote your book via inbox. Sometimes people won't buy your books because they feel they don't personally know you.

10. **Create a Facebook Fan page and tell your fans about your book-** I know we want to be humble, and it may feel strange having a fan page at first, but you'll get used to it. Promote your book on your fan page, making sure you thank everyone who has purchased your book. Always shoot to get at least three hundred fans in the first week, because fan pages with low fan counts

don't get much attention.

11. **Hold promotional events and contests**- Give away anywhere between ten to one hundred copies of your book in e-book format. Ask those who are participating to leave a review. Tell them that everyone who leaves the review will be eligible to win, for example, a gift basket.

12. **Create a press release and promote it**- Every book you write should have its own press release. You can pay someone to create one for you, or you can create it yourself.

13. **Create a website opt-in.** Give away copies of your e-book for those who opt-in through the form on your website.

Where to Make Money Selling Your Books

Below is a list of places on and offline where you can profit from selling your books:

1. **Online- Social Networking Sites and Message Boards** are great spots to promote your books.

2. **Websites** are good places to sell books, but you'll have to drive the traffic there.

3. **Online- Amazon.com** is a great place to sell books because it provides the traffic; all you need is a good marketing campaign.

4. **Local Bookstores-** Local bookstores are great places to catch readers

looking for their newest reading adventures.

5. **Local Mall-** Local malls are awesome places to catch a variety of people looking to spend a few bucks. This is a great place to learn who your target audience is, as well as perfect your marketing skills.

6. **Church or Christian Events-** Church and Christian events are really good places to market your books. Now, as far as church goes; please do not try to sell your books in church. (Remember JESUS with the whip). Instead, if your church has a bookstore, you can see about getting it listed in the bookstore.

7. **Book Clubs-** Join some local or online book clubs to promote your book. Book

clubs are full of people who absolutely love to read. This is great because it allows you to access actual readers, as opposed to people buying your book just because you asked them to. Actual readers are more active and involved with the books they read. They will often leave feedback and promote the book if it is a good read.

8. **Prisons and Shelters-** This may be alarming to many people, but prisons and shelters are great places to give away books and market at the same time. How so? The people in prisons and shelters have a lot of time on their hands, obviously; therefore, they make for good "actual" readers. They will often read your book and tell their friends and family on the outside how great your book is if it is a good read.

All the same, they aren't likely to give the book away because they'll want to read it over and over again. And the best part is, you are actually being a blessing to someone, and that's what it's all about!

Remember, the first one hundred dollars spent is to promote your book. Don't look at what's going out; understand that you are creating a runway for whatever is coming in.

Publishing Options

You can publish your book as an e-book, a print book or both. It is better to publish it in both formats, because there are people who only buy e-books, and there are some who prefer books they can hold.

Publishing your book as an e-book is less expensive than publishing it as a print book; nevertheless, most publishers have combo packages that allow for both. You will find that the e-book market has taken off in recent years; therefore, you will likely receive more e-book sales than you do print sales. All the same, there will be many who will ask for your book in print format because they don't like sitting at the computer for hours on hours reading a book. They prefer to snug up on their couches and read, so it is better to expand yourself to reach all audiences.

But what if you can't afford both right now? What if you absolutely have to choose between the two? I would recommend e-book publishing over print book publishing, and here's why: Seventy percent of my sales come from e-book purchases. The other thirty percent are from print book sales. Why do I continue to print my books then? Because print books are great for book signings and taking on the road with you. When going out and physically marketing your books, you will often sell more print books than e-books. There will be many people who say they will buy your books online once they arrive home, but they are oftentimes not being truthful. Face-to-face sales are personal, and your readers are more likely to turn into actual readers than Internet sales. You even stand the chance of selling more books offline than you do online if you actually get out and market your books.

There are many authors who make their living writing and selling e-books. Many of them do not have one book available in print. They have found this choice to be affordable and less time-consuming. Their goal is to tap into the growing e-book trend. So, it's okay to write and publish e-books only. It is a matter of preference. I prefer both ways because I love to hold my books in my hands; I love to be face-to-face with readers, and I am a publisher; therefore, I can do the work myself.

Editing Your Book

Every author should edit their own books initially. The authors who understand and do so will likely sell more books and pay less money with an editor than someone who does not. There are several reasons for this, which include; but are not limited to:

Quality of Content- You won't know if your book's content is quality content until you have reread the book from an objective point of view. As the author, you will read the book the way you intend for it to sound, but when reading the book objectively, you will read the way it actually sounds.

Self-Analysis- Reading your own books will often help you to see yourself in a different light. You'll learn things about yourself over the course of your writing career; traits and mindsets that you were unaware of before you started writing. This helps you as a writer because it teaches you to withdraw yourself from mindsets, situations and people who weigh down upon your life. For example, there are some writers who have found themselves writing countless stories about their friends and the wrongs these friends have done to them over the years. After rereading their books from an objective point of view, they recognized that these people were poisonous to their lives; therefore, they were able to disassociate themselves from these characters. This helped them as writers because they were eventually able to write more quality (and positive) content than they initially were.

Per Hour Fees- Most editors charge a per-word fee for editing; nevertheless, if your book needs excessive editing, you may be charged by the hour. Editors often charge the least for books that need proofreading or a light edit; nevertheless, if you require what is referred to as a hard edit, or line-by-line editing, you may pay up to or more than four times what you would pay for a light edit.

But how do you edit your book, and if you do edit it, why do you need to hire an editor? There are several ways to edit your book, and most authors develop their own strategies that work best for them. You need to read and edit your book from the author's point of view and an objective point of view. It is always better to self-edit your book at least three to four times before submitting it to an editor.

Self Editing

The first round of edits can be done as you write the book or after you have completed the book; it is totally up to you. The easier way, however, is to edit it as you write. Let's say you decide to write one chapter a day. After completing that chapter, you should reread it **with the intention of removing what does not read well and correcting any errors that are present.** Some authors count the text and refuse to remove problematic words, sentences, paragraphs and pages because they don't want to lose the quantity of the text; therefore, they sacrifice quality for quantity. This undoubtedly ends up costing them more sales than they will ever know.

For the first round of edits, you can read your book as it is in the word document of your choice; for example, if you are writing your book using Microsoft Word, then you can edit it from there.

The second round of edits should be an objective edit. This means you need to reread the book as if you were not the author of it.

How can you do this? It's simple; print what you have written, go into another room and reread it. Be sure to take a pen to strike through any problematic text or paragraphs. Have a notebook next to you and rewrite sentences that need to be corrected. After you are satisfied with the new line-up of words, simply transfer them into your book. Be sure to make any corrections to punctuation, and remove any run-on sentences that may be in the book. If you find yourself getting stuck at a sentence, trying to determine if it sounds right to you, rewrite it. Utilize your notebook and write that particular sentence three times using different wording. Keep the sentence that sounds best to you and transfer it into your book.

Your third round of edits should be done while reading your book in its entirety to ensure that the book flows well together. You are still looking for errors in spelling, grammar and punctuation, as well as problematic sentence structures. It is better to print the entire book and read it aloud to someone you trust. If you are married, read it to your spouse. If you are not married, read it to yourself or your children. Reading the book aloud helps you to hear what you have written, as opposed to reading it silently. Be sure to read the book sentence by sentence, taking time to address any seen issues. Take your time and read it as it is, not as you intended it to be. If you read it fast, you'll scan right past the areas that need correcting. Transfer all of the changes into your book. If you have another computer in your home, you can read it from there. Changing the computer and printing the documents off will often help you to reread the text from another point of view. In doing so, you will likely find errors that you would not have found trying to reread the editable document from the computer you are writing it at.

Finally, if you do a fourth round of edits, you would edit it from the word document itself. You would read the book in its entirety to check for errors and problematic sentence structures. Read it to yourself or read it aloud. Don't be afraid to delete paragraphs or sentences that don't work well in the book.

Editing Tricks

When editing your book, you will not see all of the errors that you have made. That's why it is better to do your first round of edits as you go along. For example, if you write three chapters tonight, you should edit those three chapters tonight. Or if the text is still too fresh for you, and you worry that you won't be able to edit it properly, try editing each day what you wrote the day before. That way, you'll be able to review the text with a fresh set of eyes.

Remember, one of the biggest misconceptions first-time authors have is that the editor will clean up their mess. Many first-timers don't properly format the text in their books; instead, they jot down notations throughout the document and they are not consistent with what they are writing. Below are three steps you can take to ensure you have a cleaner document. Please note that sending a poorly edited document to an editor actually increases the risks that your document will become a poorly edited and put together book.

Three Steps to Editing Success Using the Find Function

1. Utilize the Control + F function. You would simply hold down the control key on your keyboard, and press the "F" key. This is the "Find" function. It helps you

to find whatever it is that you are looking for. Oftentimes, what I do after I have completed the book is to check the spacing between the end of one sentence and the beginning of another. Ordinarily, I place two spaces between the end of old and the beginning of new sentences; nevertheless, I always end up putting three spaces between some of the sentences from time to time. To find and remedy this issue, I press Control + F, and I hit my space bar three times. After that, I hit enter, and I'm able to find and fix these extra spaces along the way. I also use this trick with editing.

You will also find that you have certain writing habits. For me, one of my issues used to be using "it's" instead of "its". Once I'd gotten wind of this from a couple of my editors, I began searching every document (Ctrl + F) for the word "it's" to ensure I was using it properly. You can do this every day or when you have finished your book.

Finally, always jot down your bad habits so that you can search for them once you're done. You will find that even though you intentionally try to be conscious about not making that particular mistake, you will still do it from habit.

2. If you are writing a fictional book and using characters in your book, you should use the Ctrl + F function to ensure that you haven't accidentally called one character another character's name. Believe it or not, this is super-common and often overlooked. When I wrote *Wise Her Still*, I'd called several of the characters by the wrong names somewhere in the stories. I eventually had Wise Her Still edited three times by three different editors. The first editor only caught the error once or twice, the second editor didn't catch it at all, and the third editor found numerous paragraphs where I'd mixed up the characters' names. Needless to say, I learned to search and find (Ctrl + F) each character's name and check the sentence to be sure I don't end up humiliating myself once again.

3. Another embarrassing mistake I tend to make (as well as most authors) is that I will open a quotation but forget to close it. Using the search feature, you can find every instance where you used the opening quotation mark (") and check the word or sentence to be sure you have closed the quote. Be sure to copy the quotation mark and paste it in the box that opens when you press Control

+ F. The reason is when you manually type it in, many programs pull up quotation marks that are somewhat different, and they search for those quotation marks without searching the ones you have entered manually. Especially if you have copied and pasted text into your document, you will find that some of the text has quotation marks that the search and find feature will by default locate; but if you search for what you have entered manually, it will return no results.

Reading Along or Reading Alone

As an author, it goes without saying: you want your book to be read by thousands, if not millions, of people. You didn't write it for writing's sake; you wrote it to be read. In the previous chapter, we talked about self-editing your book. This issue had to be addressed for the sake of preserving the reputation of self-published books, since self-publishing is starting to get a bad name.

When we gave the first live Remnant Writer's class, this section was not taught; nevertheless, it is important to your book's survival. What do I mean by reading along or reading alone? Think of your book as a taxi cab driver. You've paid him to take you somewhere, but instead, he keeps taking you in the wrong direction; he keeps taking you in circles, and he takes you the long way. After he's finally arrived at your destination, he wants to charge you for his errors. This is exactly what many first-time authors do. Your readers are paying you to take them somewhere, and they want a pleasant journey. They want to laugh, they want to think, and they want to be changed.

Wrong Way- Many authors have no destination marker for their books. Instead, they just write and write in hopes of finding a witty place to park. Readers, on the other hand, look for books to get better and better as they go along. If your book reads the same way it did when it started out, you have just lost yourself a reader. If you start out good, the reader expects the book to get better as they flip through the pages. Many first-time authors put their best material in the first few pages and then take the readers downhill from there.

Your book is expected to be filled with knowledge and new information that continues to ascend the reader's mind until you've reached the peak of their curiosity. From there, your readers want to reach the peak of the book; a peak that they expect to give revelation to the entire content of the book and make them want to reread the book again. Such books are considered great reads.

Going in Circles- Many authors who have no clue as to where their books are headed take their readers in circles. Confused authors kidnap the minds of their readers, taking them for long rides to nowhere. Understand that most people do not like to be confused, but many will forgive you if they feel you are going to bring them out of this confusion as the book continues to climax. If you leave them there, or take them back to where you started them off, you'll often disappoint your readers and get plenty of negative reviews. If you are writing a self-help book, make sure the advice gets better and better as you go along. If you are telling a story, make sure that the story gets better as the reader goes deeper into the pages. Each chapter should either leave the readers satisfied or leave them wanting more. Don't just take them somewhere and leave them stranded. They may find their way back to sanity and come after you with negative reviews.

Taking the Long Way- Some books are full of pages, and this is a not a bad thing if the content of the book is good and the readers' expectations are being exceeded. Nevertheless, many authors take readers on long rides for the sake of thickening up their books. It goes without saying: as authors, we want our books to be as thick as possible. But it's okay to have thin books as well. Over your writing career, you will find yourself writing thin books and books full of pages. Authors who publish one or more books a year often do just that; they write forty-page books and publish them. Now, that's forty pages as a 5x8 book, which means the actual book in word document format (8x11) is about 25 pages. The amazing part is: some of those books become best-sellers! So you don't always have to write lengthy books.

When writing a book, your readers should always be on the move to the next point in your book. Each point should satisfy something in them and cause them to hunger for more, but when you write lengthy books for the sake of having more pages in your book, you will often take your readers in circles and bring them back to where they started. Books like that are not great reads; instead, they testify against the author.

If you drop your readers off in confusion, they

will likely stay away from any future books you threaten to write. Remember, your readers are getting into your mind, and they want to be taken somewhere. Do not take them into the depths of confusion, despair and long rides with cab drivers who won't stop talking about nothing.

Thickening Up Your Book

Let's say that you want to start a book writing career: you want to write several books that you intend to print. Like any author, you want your book to be somewhat thick so your book will have a spine. But what if you want to write multiple forty-page books a year? How could you thicken up a book with such a low page count? Here are a few tips that should help you with this:

1. **Use a font such as Arial or Verdana.** Sans serif fonts tend to take up more space than serif fonts. I'll show you an example. I'll write the same sentence in both Arial and Times New Roman so you'll see the difference.

   --- Michael went to Bob's house to eat today.

--- Michael went to Bob's house to eat today. The first example of the sentence was written in Arial font, whereas the second was written in Times New Roman.

2. **Use 1.5 line spacing.** 1.5 line spacing will give you more than fifty percent more pages than single spaced lines.

3. **Add images.** You can use image inserts to describe what you are writing about and to help thicken up your book.

4. **Conduct interviews and surveys.** Adding interviews and surveys not only gives you more pages, but it gives you more readers and more insight.

5. **Publish your book as a 5x8 if necessary.** If your book is under 120 pages in length (8x10 document), you

should publish it as a 5x8 to increase the number of pages.

One of my thickest books is 378 pages long (as of today), and is a 5x8 book. The thickness makes the book look great; nevertheless, I published that book as a single-spaced book written in Times New Roman. In that book, I posted the individual results from a survey I'd given more than twenty people. Each survey alone took up about three pages. This added somewhere around sixty pages to my book. Again, the book was a single-spaced book written in Times New Roman font. Had I published it with 1.5 line spacing and Arial font, the book would have been about six hundred pages. When I write thinner books, however, I tend to do all of the above to make my books more bulky.

I worked with an author some time back who

had a book published as a 5x8, and she wanted it republished as a 6x9. She'd worked with another publisher previously to have her book published as a 5x8, but for whatever reason, she decided she wanted to redo it. When I saw the length of pages to her book, I contacted her and told her that it is better to republish the book as a 5x8, because she had about 20-25 pages in her book as a Word document. She was insistent, however, that I publish the book as a 6x9, so I did. Once the book was finished, her book had a magazine spine. The spine was just a fold, not big enough to hold any text. Needless to say, she wasn't happy with the book and requested that I republish it as a 5x8. Of course, this costs the author more money, not the publishing company. In changing the book's dimensions, the cover had to be altered, and the book had to be reformatted in its entirety. As a result, she ended up having a negative experience with my company because she refused to listen to wise counsel, and this cost everyone involved more money and time.

Right Font, Wrong Attitude

In the previous chapter, I shared a story with you of an experience I had with an author. I'd advised her to let us publish her book as a 5x8, instead of the 6x9 she was requesting, but she would not hear of it. Well, during that same publishing experience, my company ran into another issue with her. She wanted to use Comic Sans font, and I advised her against it. Needless to say, she would not listen and insisted that the book be published in Comic Sans font. I knew that she would change her mind once the book was finished, but rules are rules. She would just have to pay the change fee if that were to happen, and it did happen. Once the book was finished, and I sent it to her for review, she did not like the font. My company as well as most publishing companies will charge the customer for changes made to the font because the book has to be reformatted again.

I thought that was a one-time experience because I was a new publisher and hadn't published many books before that. That was until I was hired by another author who wanted her first book published. Again, the author sent me a document in Comic Sans font, and I warned her about using that font. I even told her of the story of the previous customer who'd used that font; nevertheless, she too insisted on using it. I was sure to let her know that if she were to request a font change after the book was formatted that she would have to pay extra, and she agreed.

Once the book was formatted and placed in the online reviewer, she hated the font. Just like her predecessor, she requested a change, but was not happy about change fees.

I share those testimonies with you to warn you against two things:
   1. Using the wrong type of font.
   2. Not listening to the professionals.

My company has published books for many authors, and ninety-eight percent of our transactions go smoothly. Nevertheless, we sometimes get that customer who wants to control the process, and they always end up spending more money because the publisher ends up having to spend more time working on their projects.

The font you choose will make or break your book. Comic Sans, for example, is a somewhat sloppy font. It looks like handwriting, and it does not look good in a serious book. It may work in a children's book;

especially if the author uses it to show dialogue between two children, but in an adult book, Comic Sans is not visually appealing.

Below is a paragraph in Comic Sans font:

Martha went to the mall to see if they'd ordered the blue sweater she wanted. Her family reunion was coming up in January, and she wanted to wear that blue sweater to set off her eyes. At the mall, Martha discovered that they not only had the blue sweater, but they had a green one just like it!

As you can see, the font isn't an ugly font, but it is not too nice to the eyes if done in an entire book. Fonts that look handwritten are not always the best choices for serious books; especially self-help Christian books.

The best fonts and font sizes for serious tones are:

Right Font, Wrong Attitude

Adobe Garamond Pro (14pt)

Arial (12 pt)

Book Antiqua (12 pt)

Bookman Medium (12 pt)

Georgia (12 pt)

Minion Pro (13 pt)

Palatino (12)

Times New Roman (12 pt)

Verdana (12 pt)

Make sure when you are choosing a font that you try it out on your entire book before sending it to the publisher. Some fonts look okay on paragraphs, but when the entire book or main body of the book is in those fonts, they look horrible. Be sure to print the page that you are testing the font on as well, and be absolutely sure that the font you have chosen is the font you are willing to live with.

If the publisher you are working with is a professional publisher, at least consider their advice. Being indifferent almost always has the same side effects: higher prices and longer waits. If you are adamant about having things done your way, you have the right to stand by what you want and get what you want. All the same, the publisher has the right to charge you extra should you change your mind if your way doesn't work out.

The publishing and editing process is normally a pleasant, yet somewhat time-consuming process. Be patient, understanding, and above all, be willing to go that extra mile if necessary to ensure your readers get the best experience possible when reading your book.

10 More No-Nos Worth Mentioning

1. Never add abbreviations to your book. Abbreviations often indicate that the writer threw the book together. Abbreviations include the all-too-popular Internet slang which includes: lol (laughing out loud), lmbo (laughing my butt off), omg (oh my gosh), ikr (I know, right) and so on. Such terms shine the author in an unprofessional light.
2. Never use slang or improper English, as it will indicate to the reader that they have just wasted their money on a bad read.
3. Never write as if you are speaking personally to the reader. For example, some writers write things like, "You know

I had to tell him the truth, right? I was just telling my cousin the other day how I felt about the situation, and do you know what he said to me?" Such statements and questioning read as if you have written a note to a personal friend rather than written a book. A better way of writing both sentences would be: "I had to tell him the truth. I spoke with a cousin of mine one day, and he said…" What I'm doing in the sentences is speaking as a writer, but not as a personal buddy who is sending a note home.

4. Never apologize for something you have written or are about to write. This is very tacky and should not be done. An example would be: "I'm sorry, but I have to tell y'all the truth, and I know some of you are going to be offended, but here goes…" Just write what you have to say

10 More No-Nos Worth Mentioning

and be done with it. The correct way to write this is, "The truth is…" and just state the truth.

5. As a Christian writer, be careful that you don't end up adding sex scenes and violent dialogues to your book. It's okay, for example, to let the reader know that sex happened without giving them the details. Christian readers are often avoiding secular books to protect themselves from the spirits therein; nevertheless, many find themselves reading pornographic books that hide under the category of a Christian book. All the same, when speaking of sex, you should either be testifying or making a point to help the reader stray away from sin. Sex scenes with no direction are just the writer's attempt to engage the readers in soft porn.

6. When you start a point, make the point.

10 More No-Nos Worth Mentioning

Remember we talked about the cab driver who took the readers in circles? Well, this is similar, but not exactly the same. Sometimes, writers will begin mentoring their audience and then share a testimony with the audience to help them better understand their point. Then, they get caught up in the testimony and start branching off into other stories and tips. Stay with the point; you can add the extra stuff later. A good example is: "It is never wise to tell a person what your plans are for life. A good example would be the time when I told a friend that I was planning to travel to Alaska. I thought she was happy for me, but I heard a recognizable silence on the other end of the phone. I knew what that meant. She was not happy, but envy had closed her mouth once again. She could not celebrate me

10 More No-Nos Worth Mentioning

because she had trouble celebrating anyone who went further than she did. As a matter of fact, I remember a story when she'd heard that her sister was going to be promoted on her job. Instead of celebrating like everyone else, she left and was missing for three days. Another time, she thought her husband had won the car that was being auctioned off at the mall, and she started yelling at him. I don't know why she is the way she is. She can be her own worst enemy." As you can see from that paragraph, we started off talking about the fact that it was unwise to share your plans with everyone. Then, we branched off into a testimony about the author's friend, and this was okay because it lined up with what we were talking about. Finally, the author's friend became the subject of the sentence, and we lost our original subject somewhere mid-paragraph. This only confuses the reader.

7. You should never demean anyone in your book. There are MANY authors who refer to people in demeaning tones because they haven't forgiven the people who hurt them, or they are angry with someone who is hurting them. If that's the issue, you definitely need to be delivered before you usher someone else towards the light of freedom. If that's not the issue, make sure your tone reflects that you have forgiven the people from your past; otherwise, you draw your readers into an ongoing conflict.

8. Make sure you use words your target audience can understand. Many authors think that they are supposed to use elaborate words when writing

books; therefore, many use words that most people can't define. This is their attempt to sound like what they perceive to be the tone of an author. What ends up happening is the reader can't get into the book because they can't understand the book. They need a translator to read the book, and no one is going to go through the trouble of having a book deciphered so they can understand it.

9. Never try to fill in your books pasting pages of text from the books of other authors. It's okay to post quotes, short paragraphs and notations from other authors, but it is never a good idea to give your readers pages and pages of that author's material. Some authors do this in an attempt to fill in their pages. If they have decided that they want their books to be one hundred pages, many authors will write 75 pages and fill in the remaining 25 pages with text from the books of others. How does this work against you? You are literally creating fans for the other author, and the reader may lose interest in what you wrote and go to purchase the author's book that you are sourcing from. Understand that your readers will either believe that the knowledge you are sharing is knowledge that is in you, or it is knowledge you have taken from someone else. No one wants secondhand information when they can get it firsthand. When posting quotes from others, it is better to post a variety of quotes from a variety of authors than it is to fill your book with quotes form one author.

10. Never use the real names of the people you are mentioning in your book, especially if your message shines them

10 More No-Nos Worth Mentioning

in a bad light. There are people out there who would love to sue you for slander. Don't grant them this opportunity. Even if they don't win, they can still use your book as a platform to write their own.

Professional Photography & Its Counterparts

Should you have a professional photo taken for the back of your book's cover? After all, the photo on the back cover is often small and many people don't pay any attention to it, right? Wrong. Many people actually do look at the image on the back cover, because people are visionaries; they like to see who wrote the book so they can get a better feel of the book.

As you have probably discovered from the content of this book, many self-published authors look for the cheap way out. Because of this, many don't seek professional photographers. Instead, the average author looks to his or her cell phone for an image of themselves that they like. They submit that photo to the publisher, asking if the background of the image could be removed. What is born is an awful book cover that looks like it was found in somebody's attic. But this won't be you, because you will know better.

The truth is images come in high and low resolutions. Any image that is going to be printed should come in three hundred d.p.i. resolution; that is, three hundred dots per image. You won't find this in many cell phones, nor will you find it in inexpensive digital cameras. You will find this, however, in many DSLR cameras. DSLR cameras are the cameras that professional photographers use. They are often the cameras with the detachable lens and the flash at the top. A good DSLR camera can run you anywhere from $599 on up. It goes without saying that many people cannot afford to purchase a professional DSLR camera, and this is why

Professional Photography and Its Counterparts

they head to a professional photographer.

It is always better to get professional photos of yourself because they make for better book covers and a better presentation. You have to consider that you may end up getting a website, a press kit, or a flyer, all of which should be done professionally. Unprofessional images often work against the author more than they work for them. I always tell authors that it is better that they had no image on their book covers than to put an unprofessional photo on the cover.

But what if you want to have that professional image, but you can't afford the typical three hundred dollars or more that most professional photographers require for studio sessions? It's simple; schedule yourself a session at your local Wal-Mart. Oftentimes, they run specials that allow you to get photos done for $7.99 or less. With these specials, you can often request that your initial photo be on a professional white background, with a close-up shot. You could even use another color for your background, as long as it is a solid color. Of course, the photographer is going to take more shots of you and try to sell them to you, but you don't have to get them; just get the $7.99 offer. The great thing about this package is you can see the photo after you take it, and you can have the photographer to retake the image. Now, if you end up in a Wal-mart with a cranky photographer who refuses to retake the photo, simply leave and come back on a day when another photographer is there.

Another way to get professional photos is to search Craigslist.org. I often help some of my clients find professional photographers in their areas by searching Craiglist. Here are a few tips for shopping Craigslist.

Professional Photography and Its Counterparts

1. If the ad seems suspicious, trust that voice in you that says to not respond to it. Don't be lured in by prices.
2. Cheap isn't always better. If you see two photographers that you want to use - one has decent photos in his portfolio and he charges $99, whereas the other has excellent photos, and he charges $149 - it is better to go with the excellent photographer. After all, you will be using your images for years to come.
3. Search "free photographer", and search "portfolio photographer". Oftentimes, you will find photographers in your area who are looking for free subjects to photograph. This is done to help the photographer build their portfolio, and it is rather common in larger cities.
4. Remember, you need a studio session, not an outdoor session. If you can't find a studio photographer in your area, it's

okay to go ahead and go with an on-location outdoor photographer. Just find somewhere you can be photographed where there is an almost solid background. A beach is a great place, when you are taking photos in front of the ocean.

5. Ask to see the photographer's portfolio. Some photographers will photograph anything, including pornographic images. You don't want to end up in a portfolio of pornography. Only work with family photographers and photographers who have morals.
6. Take someone with you. Never go to a photo shoot alone. If you are a woman, take a man with you; if you are a man, take another man with you.
7. Never take photos in a remotely hidden location, unless you are sure the photographer is a professional. Always

go to well-lit areas where there is traffic.
8. Only schedule photo sessions in the daylight hours; do not schedule any night sessions.
9. Tell the photographer what you need the images for. Some photographers would love to have the opportunity to get you out of a chair and let you be expressive in your photos. Expressive photos look better and serve many more purposes than basic, seated photos.
10. Take a few changes of clothes, if you schedule an entire session.
11. Always ask the photographer to take some shots of you wearing a color that opposes the backdrop. For example, if you are wearing all black, many photographers would want to photograph you on an all black background. This makes it almost impossible for the graphic designer to

cut your photo out, should they need to. Take some the way the photographer recommends, but also consider your graphic designer. If you are wearing all black, ask the photographer to use a white backdrop for a few of your shots.

12. Ladies, wear your hair in styles that can easily be altered. Many times, women try new hairstyles when coming to a photo session. Once the photos are printed, they find that they don't like the photos because of their hairstyles. As a photographer, I always recommend that the women wear versatile styles. That way, they can play around with their hair during wardrobe changes. This gives them a better variety of styles to choose from when they receive their photos.

13. Fellows, it's okay to smile on some photos. Every one of your photos doesn't have to look like a prison mug

shot. You may find that you like the photos of you smiling more than you like the ones of you glaring.
14. Bring props such as your Bible, sunglasses, purses to match your clothing and so on. You may want to switch it up from time to time.
15. Take some seated photos as well as some photos standing.
16. Be versatile in your posing; don't think too hard about how the image will look.
17. Call some local universities to see if they have any photographers who are looking to expand their portfolios. Many universities do have photography students, and they'll happily photograph you for free. All they ask in return is that you allow them to use your photo in their portfolios.
18. If you bring your family, remember to take some photos alone. After all, you

will only want your photo on the back of the cover.

19. Bring extra makeup, brushes and other items to help refresh you during the session.
20. Don't be stiff. Photographers are actually pretty rushed when they photograph people who are stiff and unappealing. Make the session fun, and the photographer may actually end up giving you a longer session with more photos.
21. Don't be obnoxious or bring obnoxious people with you. An irritated photographer won't care how your images come out. They will rush you through the session, without recommending poses to you.
22. Cheap sessions often involve the photographer giving you the images on a USB drive. Be sure to bring your USB

drive with you.

23. Never dominate the photographer or the photo shoot. Many times, people think they know better than the photographer, and they try to control the session. They often end up with less than great photos that remind them that they are not the professionals.

24. If you can afford to, be sure to bring a portable iron with you. Some clothes get wrinkled during the commute to the photographer, and professional cameras will often show every visible wrinkle present. Also, be careful how you transport your change of clothing. Don't ball them up or even fold them. It is better to put extra clothing on hangers and hang them up in your vehicle than it is to transport them folded up or balled up.

25. For back cover photos, it is better to

dress professionally than casually, but this is totally up to you.

You may even decide that you want the front cover to be a photo of you. In this case, you absolutely have to have a professional photograph of yourself. Remember to show personality in your photo session. Cross your arms a few times. Smile at the camera sometimes. Look away from the camera at other times. Just be fun, and just be yourself.

Warning About "New" Opportunities on the Block

It is very important that every author be aware and beware of certain people (spirits) who are attracted to authors and their works. As Christian authors, you will find that certain types of people will suddenly take an interest in you and what you are doing. Most of them will be people who either want to be an author or people who think, for some strange reason, that authors are rich. If you are sent out with the knowledge of how to become an author, without the warnings of what follows authors, you would be sent out in the wrong way.

As an author, I found myself being bombarded by emails from people who wanted to one day write a book. Many of them said that GOD told

Warning About "New" Opportunities On the Block

them they would write a particular book someday, and others said they just wanted to write "a" book; nothing specifically, they just wanted to be an author.

As time went on, I found that if I responded to their emails, I would get more and more emails, followed by phone numbers so that we could "connect". When I was an immature writer, I bit this line a few times and found myself being reeled into someone's attempt to drain me of all that I knew. People will ask questions about writing a book, tell you what they have written so far, and finally, worst of them all, they will try to slowly take the text from within your book to place it in their own. Ask any author, and they will likely tell you that they have come in contact with this character (spirit). Slowly but surely, their books will begin to come together, but the knowledge won't be their own. The knowledge won't be knowledge

Warning About "New" Opportunities On the Block

given to them by GOD either; it will be whatever information you have shared with them, or it may knowledge that you published in your own book. The only difference is they will slightly change the text to make it their own. Before you know it, they will have rewritten your book, published it under a different name, and added their name as the author. After that, you will be of no use to them.

Almost every author I have come in contact with has been inundated by emails from people who had this wicked and envious spirit attached to them. Many of them did make the mistake of "connecting" with these characters, only to find themselves on the other end of legal plagiarism. I refer to it as legal plagiarism because individuals who often write books using the ideas of others won't write it word-for-word; they'll write the book in their own text.

Warning About "New" Opportunities On the Block

This makes it difficult, if not impossible, to prove that your book has been plagiarized. All the same, some people won't actually take the information from your published books; they will take the information from conversations they have had with you; conversations where you told them about new books you intended to write. After you share it, they will start writing that book immediately.

As a first-time author, you need to know this so that you won't fall prey to this character. Here are a few tips to help you avoid this character, and any other spirit that may attempt to siphon information out of you.

1. Do you remember the adage, "There is nothing free in America?" That is somewhat of a fact. There are people who will offer to do "free" work for your book because they believe so dearly in the success of your book. Understand

Warning About "New" Opportunities On the Block

that it isn't as "free" as you think it is. Beware of characters who insist on promoting for you freely. Some may truly believe in the success of your book, but most (and I do mean most) have hidden, if not public, agendas.

2. Beware of people who want to use lines from your book and publish them in their own. Now, it's not a bad thing for someone to want to use a powerful quote or point that you made, as long as they reference you in their books. Nevertheless, most people who ask for this aren't looking to reference you; they are looking to take credit for whatever you said. That's why you will find that the majority of people who ask for this will often rewrite what you said in their own words.

3. After you have written a book, you will have new knowledge of the writing and publishing process. It's a great idea to help others to write their books if you desire to do so, but be careful that you don't become a free and unwitting coach. I have met people who have become free agents, and most of them weren't so happy about their new and unofficial roles. Remember this: You can charge for what you know. If someone wants to use you as a coach, tell them your coaching fees. When you charge for coaching, many people will come in and try to wear the disguise of a "friend". From there, they will ask for information little by little, until they feel they've gotten what they need from you. Always keep your conversations to friends on a "friendly" note. When they start to talk business, send them an invoice. Attempts to get free information often start off with, "I have a quick question." This usually indicates that the person asking the question does understand that you charge for coaching; nevertheless, if they can ask for a little bit of coaching here and there, they feel they won't have to pay you. If you notice that a friend is slowly bleeding you of information that you charge others for, slowly or abruptly stop taking their calls.

4. Beware of characters who attempt to show you "better" ways that your book could have been written. Oftentimes, people will try to insert their own words in your book and then use those words in their own books. This is an attempt to credit themselves with your words in their own terms. Don't get me wrong, some people do this out of love with no expectation; nevertheless, there are many platform-seekers on the prowl,

and they love new authors.

5. Beware of aspiring authors who offer to partner with you in writing a book. If you are new and have not written a book yet, this can be good if GOD gives you the green light. Nevertheless, if you have already published a book, especially if you have garnered any success or recognition from that book, there will be many who will offer to co-write a book with you. This is an attempt to gain recognition from the very audience who follows your work. Even if you haven't written a book and someone offers to co-author with you, don't jump on the offer right away. Always pray about it and wait for GOD'S answer first and foremost. Understand that there are MANY aspiring authors who will only aspire to write because they don't want to cough up the money

for publishing a book. They will often offer to co-write with other authors in an attempt to save themselves some money. Authors who fall into these schemes often end up being the major contributors in both the writing and financing of the books; nevertheless, they bind themselves legally to their co-authors, and this never has a happy ending. Finance your own books; let GOD give you the platform HE has for you, and only accept to co-author with whomever GOD leads you to co-write with.

6. Beware of people who want to add your name to their books for no apparent reason. Some authors find themselves "flattered" not understanding that a flattering tongue (according to the Bible) is a wicked thing. Please know that there are many people out who are seeking platforms, and they will use your name in an attempt to share one with you....if you let them.

7. Copyright your book legally at copyright.gov. Also be sure to have a cease and desist letter on hand at any given time. It is better to warn potential threats before you have to go through the painstaking task of hiring a lawyer to sue them.

8. Separate your professional life as a writer from your personal life. You will find that if you insistently separate the two, most people who see you as a platform will get away from you in haste. When someone tries to talk about your book, it's okay to talk about the book as if you are trying to sell it to them. If they want to talk about the creation of your book, tell them that you don't discuss the planning, production or promotion of

your books. After that, change the conversation; otherwise, many will want to elaborate on your reason for not sharing, as well as try to reason with you to share.

9. Beware of individuals who say they can connect you with well-known figures. These characters come a dime a dozen, and they more than likely don't know nor are they connected to the people they claim to know and be connected to. Even if they were, how could this help you? I have come across many authors who excitedly told me about someone who said they knew certain well-known figures, and they would tell these celebs about the author's book. I would warn the author, of course, because these characters are everywhere. It goes without saying that by the next time I'd see the author, his or her attitude will

Warning About "New" Opportunities On the Block

> have changed about their hopeful connection. People who do this are actually attempting to either use you as a platform to exalt themselves higher than they perceive you are, or to get something out of you. The key is to understand again and again that no one will bring success to you; GOD will promote you, not man.

I wanted to share this not-so-practical information because this is TRULY what happens to many Christian authors, and it is rarely discussed. The reason it is not discussed much is because many authors think that such instances only happened to them. Needless to say, when they get around other authors who are open to share their experiences as an author, they learn that their experiences mirrored someone else's. I'm sure it happens to secular authors as well, but I

Warning About "New" Opportunities On the Block

have only worked in the Christian realm with authors. You need to be aware of sudden opportunities and any attempted connections that seem rushed or too good to be true. What I'm about to share with you will save you time, money and unnecessary legal battles: No one will usher you towards success but GOD. Don't trust in any connections; don't trust in yourself, and don't honor man to the point where you think that they can help you sell your books. As an author, you are simply building an audience of readers initially. Your second book will help to sell your first book; your third book will help to sell your second book and so on. That's just the way it works. Don't waste valuable time investing your trust in a bunch of people who couldn't help themselves, let alone help you. You should simply write whatever GOD told you to write, and let success find you in obedience. You will see countless authors jumping on sinking ships with other authors in an attempt to gain recognition, but you will also see that one lone author who just writes books and advertises what they have written. You will notice that the lone author has found more success alone than those who kept searching for ways to find success in numbers. A good and faithful author won't try to find their success in group settings; instead, they will let their work speak for them. It's not bad to co-author a book. As a matter of fact, I recommend that you do co-author a book with someone, but always make sure that those who you co-write with are already just as established as you are as an author, and your motives are to write books that bless the people of GOD.

There are many authors on the scene, and more than half of them lean to their own understanding. They look long and hard for success, and this opens them up to every type

Warning About "New" Opportunities On the Block

of wicked soul and scheme alive. Other people have no trouble seeing how blessed you really are, even when you can't. You will not find success in people; I can't elaborate on that enough. You will be found by success when you are faithful, persistent and obedient to GOD. Anything else that looks like success is just a mirage.

Tips For Writing a Great Fictional Book

A lot of Christian authors are taking to storytelling. While some make for great fictional writers, others do not. Here are a few tips to help you along the way in your writing.

1. Make a list of character names before you start the book. This will help you to stay focused on the story and not become distracted by finding names for your characters.
2. If you need a name mid-sentence, Google what you are searching for.
3. Give details about the characters. Your readers want to know what the characters look like, what they smell like and how they carry themselves. Give the readers a visual image of the

character by giving them a detailed description.
4. Tell the readers how the characters are feeling at any given time. If Jane is a character in your story, for example, and she found out that her sister was the thief who stole her money, talk about how she felt. Many authors will tell you how Jane reacted, but a good author will go into depth about what caused Jane to react.
5. Talk about the characters' surroundings at any given time. Remember, the readers are reading and imagining what you are talking about. Don't make them do all of the work trying to create a scene or a mood.
6. Talk about how the characters' surroundings affected them. For example, saying that Robert was running through the tall grass trying to

get away from the bear that was chasing him is good. Telling the readers how the environment affected Robert is better. A good example is: "As Robert ran through the tall grass, he could feel the moisture underneath his feet. The blades of grass seemed sharp; so sharp that some of the blades cut away at his skin. His pants began to fall away from his waste. He tugged at his pants to hold them up so that he could get away from the angry mother bear, who seemed to be gaining ground on him. He could hear her pants as she struggled to catch her breath." What you are doing is giving the reader a visual and helping them to live vicariously through the character.

7. Make sure every character is vital to the story. Don't introduce pointless characters who don't shape or direct the

story. Adding extras is okay, but they don't necessarily have to have names unless it is vital to the story. All too often, an author will have a name that they want to incorporate into the story. Having no place for the character, they insert some insignificant character into the story who does not add to the story, but often ends up taking away from it. Don't do this. If you have a character name that you just have to use, use it in your next story.

8. Give each character a name that's readable. Never give character names that your readers may have trouble pronouncing.
9. Don't engage your characters in pointless dialogues.
10. Remember every scene should lead to the next scene. Every inch of your book should draw the reader in further and

further. Every dialogue should explain or set up the next scene.

11. Leave nothing left unexplained. Each reader is different. Some readers will want to know what happened in one set, whereas another reader may want to know what's going to happen in another set. You can let the text be mysterious, leading each reader clue by clue further into the book, but you will have to explain what's going on in every set before you end the book. Readers left unsatisfied leave bad reviews. Also explain things little-by-little as you go along. It's like dropping crumbs along the way, so that your readers won't starve trying to get to the whole point.

12. Don't be so obvious. If your book reads like a mystery, let it be just that...a mystery. Your readers should not be able to easily figure out how the book

Tips For Writing a Great Fictional Book

will end, which character is good or bad, or how each scene will play out. The element of surprise makes for a good read.

13. Make sure that all of your characters have their own personalities. Many times, authors give each character a part of their own personalities, and the characters end up all sounding alike. Make sure your book's characters are all different, even if they are twins. Show the difference in their personalities and choices.

14. Don't be overly dramatic. Some authors overdo it and create unrealistic stories that overwhelm the readers' imaginations in the wrong way. Remember, your book should read like an ocean: at times, there is calm, and at other times, there are storms overhead.

15. Don't kill the main character. Many

authors do this, but you have to understand that your readers will often become drawn into the main character; many of them will become the main character in their own minds. Readers are often bothered by the killing of someone they have grown to like. Now, if the main character must die, make sure there is a point to it and a happy ending because of it.

16. Don't villianize the main character. Always remember that your readers will often take the character's place and make themselves a part of your story. If you make the main character a villain, they won't be able to relate to him or her, nor will they want to place themselves in the character's shoes.

17. Let GOD be glorified in the book. You are writing a Christian book; right? Therefore, you are committing to glorify

the LORD with your book. Don't write stories where Satan wins, because he never wins.

18. Never switch the main characters out. Not too many authors do this, but just in case someone considers it, please don't do it.
19. Don't list your dialogue in paragraphs. If the characters in the story are having an extensive dialogue, be sure to list each dialogue line-by-line.

Wrong Way: She asked, "Malcolm, what are you doing?" Malcolm responded, "What do you think I'm doing? I'm calling your mother!" Stunned, she asked, "Why would you do that?" To that, Malcolm responded, "Because I can."

Right Way:

Denise: Malcolm, what are you doing?

Malcolm: What does it look like I'm

doing? I am calling your Mother.
Denise was stunned.
Denise: Why would you do that?
Malcolm: Because I can.

No reader wants to keep reading "he said" and then "she said."

20. When writing a dialogue between multiple characters, it is better to bold the name (like I did in number 18) so the readers can easily jump from one line to the next. Sometimes, your readers may look away, and when they turn back to start where they left off, they will often find themselves lost. Make it easier for them: bold the names.

There are many things to remember when writing a fictional story, but the most important rule is: Don't just write a story; let your story tell a story. In doing so, you will engage the

Tips For Writing a Great Fictional Book

readers and reach a whole new depth of writing that you didn't know you could reach.

Your Self-Published Problem

While self-published books have become popular, they have also earned a bad reputation along the way. Many major retailers refuse to stock self-published books on their shelves, making it harder for self-published authors to sell their books. This issue stems from the fact that anybody can self-publish a book, and I do mean anybody. The fact that anyone can publish a book doesn't seem like a problem until you actually purchase a badly written, poorly edited book. Customers are understandably upset and often demand refunds when they are the unfortunate pickers of a bad book; and who could blame them? After all, you read the book's synopsis, listen to all the hype the author has published about the book, and you take the risk in buying that book. Instead of getting a book worth reading, you end up with a book worth burning. The funny part is, people who write horrible books often want the most money for their books. People who refuse to pay for editors have no problem writing a good and clean synopsis to draw the readers in; nevertheless, their books are filled with run-on sentences, misspelled words and pointless dialogues. They did what they set out to do: they wrote a book, even though it wasn't a very good book.

Now it's your turn to write your self-published book, and like most first-time authors, you will be tempted to save money by doing most of the work yourself. After all, how hard could it be? You will think about editing your own book or having a family member or friend edit your book. You will think about going with a plain, free cover design that you could put together online. You will think about publishing your own book. You will basically think about becoming your book's own worst enemy.

It's okay to ponder on ways to save money, but it is always better to ponder on ways to birth out a professional book worth looking at and reading. After all, once your book is written, it belongs to whomever buys it. Why sell them something you wouldn't want to buy in your sober state of thinking? Why sell them mountains of text that have no peak? That is to say to you: Don't be a part of a growing statistic. Be one of the few people who actually publishes a professionally put together and written book.

When I published my very first book, *The Gospel Propeller*, I was elated with the idea of being an author. I didn't know that most retailers would refuse to stock my book because it was self-published; I didn't know that I absolutely had to have an editor; I didn't know that my cover should be professional; I thought my cover should be cute. I wrote the book in a day or two and published it. I wasn't a very good graphic designer at the time, so I put together what I thought was a cute cover according to my skill set. It was atrocious, and the book, while a good read, was full of errors and attempts at wit. Not to mention, the cover design and formatting was just all wrong. A year or so later, I wanted to do it all over again. After all, I was still proud of my first book, so I decided to write a cookbook called *The Anointed Cookbook*. Even though my skills as a graphic designer had improved by then, I was still not where I needed to be to create a book cover. Nevertheless, I created the cover, slapped my face on it and smiled when the book arrived in the mail. I was so proud to hand those atrocities over to people. That is until I learned better. Who needs an editor? My thoughts were: Editor-creditor; they both want money. That was my line of thinking until I would go through my books and find errors upon errors.

When I wrote my third book, I still wasn't quite convinced that I needed an editor. I wrote a powerful book called *The Spirit of Heaviness and All Its Cousins*. I threw the cover together (and I was proud of it), and I published it using an online printing company who ended up printing this horrid stack of books and sending them to me. I'd ordered one hundred copies, and not one time did this company say to me that my formatting was wrong, my book needed a re-working, or that I should consider getting an editor. How did they know I needed an editor? The name I had splashed on the cover of my book was *The Spirit of Heaviness and All It's Cousins*. That was all wrong! The word "it's" means "it is"; therefore, the name of my book was *The Spirit of Heaviness and All It Is Cousins*. I didn't figure this out until a man on Facebook pointed it out to me in my comments. I was humiliated; my book had been selling for almost a year, and here I was using the word "it's" throughout the book when I was supposed to be using "its". All the same, it wasn't the printer's job to point these things out to me, even though I would as a publisher. So, I ended up with a box of books that I was too ashamed to sell. That was three hundred bucks gone down the hole. I was so upset with the printer that I ended up leaving them a bad review, even though most of their customers song them praises. I felt great to see that another customer or two had shared the same experience that I had shared and was giving them negative feedback as well; nevertheless, as time went on, I learned that most (if not all) printers would do the very same thing. I went ahead and hired an editor for *The Spirit of Heaviness and All Its Cousins*, redesigned the cover and republished the book professionally. It's up to you to decide whether you want to be professional or not. It's up to you whether you decide to hire an editor or not. It's up to you to decide whether you will invest in your book or not. But understand that when the tables turn, and your book is in the stores, it is up to your readers whether they want to invest in your book or not.

As a publisher, I have had people send me books that needed to be edited. When formatting the book, I see words like "it's" where "its" should have been. I see misspelled words, jargon and run-on sentences; nevertheless, I can only recommend to the author that they hire an editor. Of course, I do this before we start formatting the book for publishing. When the author insists that the book has been reviewed by themselves or others, I have to leave the situation alone and do what they are paying me to do. If I don't, I'll lose the customer, and they'll find someone else who will happily publish their books. I can't tell them that they misspelled "it's", because they would assume I am going to edit their entire book. I have had people hire me to publish their books say to me, "If you find any spelling or grammatical errors in my book, feel free to correct them." Of course, I had to tell them that they would need to hire me as an editor before I could do this. Now, it goes without saying, if I saw the title misspelled, I would have to say something.

My box of one hundred books became my self-published problem, and not the printer's. Sadly enough, more than half of the self-published authors coming on the scene now will replicate my errors and find themselves out of hundreds, if not thousands, of dollars trying to save a few bucks.

You need an editor; you can't go without one. At the same time, you need a good editor. When I finally started going with editors, I searched high and low online for editors. I found and hired a woman who referred to herself as a perfectionist, and she ended up doing a slight edit on a few pages and then abandoning the project. For months upon months, I would write her, and she would tell me she was going through some hardships. Other times, she told me she was out of town. Finally, I got tired of waiting and had to hire a new editor. I didn't like the way the missing in action editor edited anyhow, because she was changing the way I spoke to fit how she felt I should speak. Even though I was publishing my fourth book, and my writing was still tainted with failed attempts to be witty, I felt she was deleting more than half of the text I wrote.

I hired another editor, and I felt so blessed to have her. At that time, I was under the assumption that editors were perfect, and they'd find every issue in a manuscript. I didn't want to reread my book, but the LORD weighed heavy on my heart to do so. When I reread the edited book, I was horrified. I found errors upon errors that had been overlooked. I didn't want to write her off as a bad editor, so I sent my book to another editor after I cleaned up the errors I saw. The next editor found countless mistakes throughout the book. I was convinced that the book was finally error-free, but I was wrong. After rereading the book again, I found a few more errors, but not a lot. Over the years, I have tried many editors and have found that there is no such thing as a perfect editor. Editors often rank (by my experience) as bad, typical, good or great.

Your Self-Published Problem

When my husband came back and told me that one of his managers said he'd paid an editor six thousand dollars to edit a book, and he'd still found errors, I was surprised. I'd only paid four hundred dollars or less for every book of mine, depending on the size of my book. After trying on so many editors, I finally found one or two who I rated as great editors. To this day, I only stick with the great editors unless GOD tells me otherwise. This is to say that you need to hire an editor and go back and reread your book after it has been edited. That way, you can catch any errors that the editor missed, and you will know whether or not you want to work with that editor again. If you are not good with writing, ask someone you know to reread the book for you. Once your book is published, it becomes your self-published problem.

Another revelation I came across when hiring an editor is the fact that a good editor doesn't always cost you an arm and a leg. That's a misconception that many people have fallen victim to, including myself at some point in my writing career. You will come across websites who advertise "perfect" editors for high prices; and then again, you will come across people who edit from the comforts of their own homes. Which one should you choose? The average person would want to go with the company who charges the most, but the reality is that being high priced doesn't mean the editor is good. As a matter of fact, you will find that many high priced editors aren't charging you because of their skill level; they are charging high prices because they absolutely hate editing books. They can edit a book, but it isn't something they are passionate about. Since they hate editing books, you will have to pay them up to ten times as much as you would have to pay an editor who was passionate about their craft. They appear to be good

Your Self-Published Problem

editors, but they are not. For example, the woman who took my money had a head full of white hair, and she reported that she was once a school teacher. I thought I was in good hands, but I soon found out that she had pet peeves. They weren't actual problems with grammar or spelling, they were little issues that were annoying to her. One thing she hated was the use of the words "this" or "that". She preferred that I say what "this" or "that" meant, even if I'd just indicated what the subject was in the previous sentence. A good example is: "Jason couldn't find his wallet. This angered him and he went to file a police report." We know that "this", as used in the sentence above, meant the fact that Jason couldn't find his wallet; nevertheless, it was a pet peeve for her.

I was too busy looking at her exterior, and the fact that she'd been a school teacher, that I never took into consideration the fact that she could be a bad editor or even take my money. I don't know if she was a bad editor because she never completed the work; she took my money and ran. All the same, she seemed frustrated with the few pages that she did edit. Her notes to me sounded rude and teacher-like, but I forgave her easily because I knew she had once been a teacher. Her notes read like, "I told you not to use the word "this" in place of the subject. Go back through your document and make the changes. I will not correct this problem again."

In looking for an editor, you need to remember that high-priced doesn't always mean professional. The best editors that you can find will be the ones who are passionate about reading books. These are the characters who love to read and are disturbed when they see a misplaced comma. They are often pleasant to work with, and they are often inexpensive in comparison to other editors. That's because they love what they do, and it doesn't feel like work to them.

Be sure to shop around, and don't allow yourself to feel as if you need to stay with a particular editor. It is good to shop around until you find one or two who are friendly and passionate about what they do.

Another issue is formatting. My husband and I were in Wal-Mart getting an oil change, and the tech told us that our car would be ready in an hour or so. To burn time, we just walked around the store looking for anything that would catch our interest. I found myself being drawn to the book section, and my eyes fixated on the inspirational books. Inspirational is just retail's way of saying "Christian" books. Anyhow, I began to flip through the books, looking at their book's setup and getting ideas as I went along. I found that about forty to fifty percent of the books sitting on the shelf were not professionally formatted, even though they'd been published by some of today's most prolific publishers. I was surprised, to say the least. How is it that Wal-Mart, and other major retailers, refuse to list self-published books, when they had shelves and shelves of books that were formatted the wrong way? Of course, the answer is: Wal-Mart is not going to hire people to read a self-published book to ensure that it is properly written. I picked up book behind book, and I kept showing my husband the formatting problems. Of course, he doesn't publish books, so he took my word for it.

When you decide to publish your book, be sure to check the publisher's portfolio. It is wise to buy books that were published by the publisher you intend to use. That way, you can get a feel for their work and determine whether or not you want to work with them. At the same time, you could compare books published by several publishers. Sure, you'd spend a few bucks ordering the books, but it's money well spent. If you don't invest in a good publisher, your book will take the hit, and it will become your self-published problem. A publisher doesn't care if you have changed your mind about the book's formatting, as long as you are willing to pay the publishing fees all over again. The goal is to get your book done right the first time, rather than being handed a published catastrophe that no one wants to read. People who try to find the cheap way out often find themselves paying double what others have paid for a professional. That's because they go about it the cheap way initially and soon realize that they absolutely have to hire a professional and do it all over again.

Finally, you must remember not to get so hyped up about becoming a millionaire. There are countless authors out there who are writing books for the sole purpose of becoming a millionaire, and the truth hits these authors the hardest. I have ran into plenty of bitter authors who brazenly recount how little sales they have made, and I have listened to them go on and on about how they will never support their friends, family members and other authors. They had visions of dollar signs dancing in their heads, but they were soon awakened to the reality that publishing a book is not a rich man's claim to fame. Many authors became well-recognized from their ministries, and THEN the people went back and started buying their books years later. Even then, many of them are not millionaires, or even close to being millionaires. Writing Christian books should be done because GOD told you to write them and because you want to help others to overcome whatever strongholds, demons and mindsets that once bound you. Remember, authors rarely make the money back they have invested in their books; **however**, this is because many don't invest much. All the same, most authors who have found success in writing books didn't find this success until they'd written more books over the years. So, if you are thinking about becoming an author because you want to be rich, you are in for a rude awakening.

The gist of it is: Come out swinging like you know your book is a best-seller. Imagine your book going far, and work towards where you want to be, not where you think you are. More than fifty percent of self-published Christian authors will throw together a book and publish it in the name of being cheap. As discussed earlier, there are ways to save money, but it is better to spend a little more now to get a lot more later. A book will not return what you did not invest. It's just like buying land; sometimes, you have to make a large investment to get a large return. If you buy a small lot, you will receive a small return. If you buy an acre, you will see a bigger return. If you believe GOD gave you that book to write, you should have no problem investing in that book. To save money, you need to shop around, and that takes time. Don't hire the first Christian editor who impresses you; don't hire the first publisher who makes the process seem easier, and don't hire the first cover design who shows you their portfolio. Take your time and let GOD lead you. Over the years, if you continue to write, you will find that you will save more money when writing and publishing your books. You will become wiser, and you will learn the tricks and the trades of self-publishing. But this guide will help you to debut yourself as an author the right way, rather than coming out the way many self-published authors come out: low-budget looking. Your appearance and your book's appearance will make a huge impact on how your book sells. Be sure to focus more on the content of your book, however, as opposed to the fact that you're about to be an author. Authors who spend too much time soaking in their soon-to-be titles often write horrible books.

Faking a Climax

One of the misconceptions that many Christian authors have is they believe their books must go out with a bang; therefore, they try to heighten the book as it nears a close. In more than fifty percent of the books I have edited, I noticed a trend with exclamation points and "emotional" words added to stir up the reader; nevertheless, neither of the two have their intended effects. Instead, they turn what would have been a bad book into an even worse read.

As I near the final pages of a book, I find that many books tend to get worse and worse. There are often more exclamation points added than I care to count. It is as if the reader is faking the climax, because they didn't reach

Faking a Climax

their point. Instead, many authors try to trick the readers into believing the book has peaked, but if they (the readers) aren't stirred up, they have obviously missed the move of GOD. Nevertheless, most readers are avid readers; therefore, they aren't tricked by this. Instead, they become even more angry with the author for wasting their time and trying to fake a climax with exclamation points.

Don't get me wrong; there are some anointed men and women of GOD out there, but they just have to learn how to write. You don't write the same way that you preach. As a writer, you have to know which voice to turn on at any given time. You have your "preacher's voice" that you use in the pulpit, and you have your "writer's voice" that you use when you write. They are not one in the same.

One of the most common errors for Christian

authors is taking their readers in a circle over and over again in their books. They say the same thing repeatedly, and then close the book out with the same message; just different words. As the book nears the end, the authors attempt to heighten the mood of the reader by adding exclamation points and emotional words. You should NEVER do this in your book; instead, you are to simply write the book and let GOD tell the story or give the message through you. Here are a few tips to help you along your writing journey:

1. **Remove all of the exclamation points and make your point.** Don't scream at your readers; they can't hear you! Ten thousand exclamation points on a piece of paper has less sound than an ant walking across that paper. Nobody wants to read sentences that end like this!!! Instead of trying to stir the reader

up, simply tap into the heart of GOD when you write. You will find that when you do, HE is a much better speaker than you are. HE will give you a message that can be subtle, but potent enough to deliver every reader who reads it. Powerful messages aren't guarded on every side by exclamation points; powerful messages are clothed with the glory of GOD and filled with HIS power. All the same, powerful messages are often followed by periods because the writer's point is made, and the message is powerful enough.

2. **Don't save your best for last.** This is a common foe of the Christian writer as well. You may have this powerful message that you want to give, and you decide that it's going to be in the last chapter of your book. This means you are trusting in your own works and

intellect and you have already decided the height of your book. In doing this, you leave GOD out. Instead, insert the message wherever GOD tells you to insert it and just trust HIM. If HE doesn't tell you to put it at the beginning of your book, then definitely don't do that either. Instead, just flow and let the message you want to insert find its own place as you write. If it ends up as the final chapter, so be it.

3. **Statistics make for great endings.** When you poll a few stats and write out the results, your readers will be captivated. The height of your book must be higher than the center of your book. That is; the end of your book should have more height and depth; it should bring the entire book to a head, and explain so many mysteries that the book has held. This doesn't mean your

book has to go out with a bang; it simply means it should satisfy the hunger of your reader. If you satisfy their hunger, they will walk away happy, but if you fill them up with new knowledge, they will follow your books for a lifetime. When polling stats, always relate them to what the Bible says, and always explain any text in your book that is left unexplained.

4. **Trust GOD.** When I wrote the book *Wise Her Still*, I had no idea how that book was going to go. Initially, I'd planned it to be a book of wise quotes, but GOD had other plans. As the book unfolded, I found myself writing stories and explaining what happened. As the book inched and inched towards the end, I didn't have to come up with this big bang to take the book out. I just wrote what GOD laid on my heart and HE did the rest. That book turned out to

be one of my highest-selling, highest-rated and most talked about books. The point is: You don't have to put too much thought into something when you are being led by GOD. All you have to do is show up at the computer and be obedient to HIS voice. Remember this: The worst books are the books written by man; the best ones are the ones written through man by GOD.

5. **Don't be afraid to keep writing if you aren't where you planned to be yet.** The issue with many writers is they plan to write a certain amount of chapters or pages for their books. Once they reach their planned limits, they stop even though the book hasn't really peaked yet. Most seasoned authors have gotten to this point at some point in their writing careers, and they have all learned this truth: if you stop writing

Faking a Climax

when your plans tell you to keep writing, your book will end up being a paperback mess full of pointless text and riddles. If your book hasn't peaked yet, you're obviously not finished with it.

6. **Clean the book up and then continue.** Sometimes, what keeps a book from being completed is irrelevant text and chapters somewhere in it. A book is like a road to a particular destination. If you take the wrong direction, you won't arrive where you have intended to arrive; instead, you will ride around in circles trying to get back on the road you were traveling. When you find yourself going in circles, you need to go back and review your book. You will often find that somewhere along your journey, you took a wrong turn with your text. Correct the issue and start again.

7. **Maybe the book did peak, but you**

haven't noticed it because it's your book. As authors, we are oftentimes our worst critics besides Satan. We expect to wow ourselves out of our seats, and we expect to be moved by our own text to the point where we can only conclude that the book is great. Many times when an author thinks their book has gone out with a bang, they are wrong. In many of those cases, the author simply found something out that they didn't know and added it to their books. They concluded that the book was great because they learned something while researching. At the same time, many authors who think their books have not peaked have written some pretty powerful books that have peaked more than one time. The issue is the author just doesn't see it because they are still looking for something to stir them up emotionally, and when it doesn't happen, they conclude that they aren't finished yet. One good idea is to copyright your book and then let a few people read it. Give it to people who love to read and ask for their honest opinion.

Remember, how good a book is isn't determined by how many exclamation points and "hallelujahs" that you add to the final chapter; it is determined by the knowledge GOD serves through you and how you season it. If you season it with flesh, you'll ruin it; if you season it with love, the readers will enjoy it over and over again.

If you have already started writing a book, go back through it and clean it up. Again, don't count how much text you have because you'll find it difficult to delete pages of text; instead, count how many readers you will lose by keeping that text. It is better to publish a forty page book full of wisdom, knowledge and understanding than it is to publish a three hundred page book full of words with no depth.

Helpful Links

Press Releases

www.prlog.org

www.prweb.com

www.pr.com

Writing Tools

www.openoffice.org

Buy Scrivener Here:

www.literatureandlatte.com

Buy Microsoft Word Here:

www.microsoft.com

Book Publishing/ Services

www.afcpublish.com

www.remnantwriters.com

Learn to Publish Your Own Books

Helpful Links

www.afcpu.com

Tools For Editing
www.whitesmoke.com

Spelling and Grammar Check Here:

spellcheckplus.com

Children/ Adult Names For Fiction Books or Disguising Characters

Girls

baby-names.familyeducation.com/popular-names/girls

Boys

baby-names.familyeducation.com/popular-names/boys

Excerpt from The Golden Book of Selling and Marketing Books

1. Go to the mall or the location where your target audience frequents. Conduct a survey by stopping twenty to forty <u>friendly</u> faces. Hand them the paper and ask them to choose the titles that they would be more likely to purchase. Ask them to pick the five that they would prefer, listing them in the order in which they would prefer them. If they are in a hurry, ask them to take the paper home with them and email the answers to you. Let them know that you will send them a free copy of your new book (in e-book format) once it's

Excerpt from The Golden Book of Marketing

    published. *(Be sure to get their email addresses, ensuring them that you won't spam them).*

2. Tally up the results and use the names that the people like the most. Tallying is easy. Give ten points to each number one choice, seven points to the number two choice, five points to the number three choice, three points to number four choice, and one point to number five choice.

(Insert: Before printing the list, research and make sure that those names aren't already listed to an author).

Excerpt from The Golden Book of Marketing

Check out the example below:

Book Name	Total # 1 Votes	Total Tally
The Relationship Guidance Counselor	6	60
Love With No Limits	1	10
An Attitude Change- When A Relationship Breaks Down	5	50
Marry Me Or Else	5	50
The Ex- Terminator- Trying To	4	40

Excerpt from The Golden Book of Marketing

Avoid Becoming An Ex		
The Dog Ate My Relationship	2	20
How To Repair A Damaged Relationship	1	10
Breaking Up With The Idea Of Breaking Up	2	20
A Relationship With No Signal- Can You Hear Me Now?	3	30

Excerpt from The Golden Book of Marketing

The Relationship Mechanic	11	110

Your chart can be more elaborate, listing the total number of votes for each category, if you so choose.

www.ingramcontent.com/pod-product-compliance
Lightning Source LLC
Chambersburg PA
CBHW071244160426
43196CB00009B/1152